As I open this book,
I open myself
to God's presence
in my life.

God's Invitation

God calls me
to be aware of him
in all the people I know,
the places I go,
and the things I do each day.

My Response

When I quiet myself to allow
God's grace to help me,
I see with truth,
hear with forgiveness,
and act with kindness
as God's love works through me.

Thank you God,
for your presence
in my life.

Finding God

Our response to God's gifts

1

Parish Edition

Barbara F. Campbell, M.Div., D.Min.
James P. Campbell, M.A., D.Min.

LOYOLA PRESS.
A JESUIT MINISTRY
Chicago

Nihil Obstat **Reverend John G. Lodge, S.S.L., S.T.D.** **Censor Deputatus** **March 6, 2004**	*Imprimatur* **Most Reverend Edwin M. Conway, D.D.** **Vicar General** **Archdiocese of Chicago** **April 14, 2004**	**The Ad Hoc Committee to Oversee the Use of the Catechism, United States Conference of Catholic Bishops, has found this catechetical series, copyright 2005, to be in conformity with the *Catechism of the Catholic Church.***

The *Nihil Obstat* and *Imprimatur* are official declarations that a book is free of doctrinal and moral error. No implication is contained therein that those who have granted the *Nihil Obstat* and *Imprimatur* agree with the content, opinions, or statements expressed. Nor do they assume any legal responsibility associated with publication.

***Finding God: Our Response to God's Gifts* is an expression of the work of Loyola Press, an apostolate of the Chicago Province of the Society of Jesus.**

Senior Consultants

Jane Regan, Ph.D.
Richard Hauser, S.J., Ph.D., S.T.L.
Robert Fabing, S.J., D.Min.

Advisors

Most Reverend Gordon D. Bennett, S.J., D.D.
George A. Aschenbrenner, S.J., S.T.L.
Paul H. Colloton, O.P., D.Min.
Eugene LaVerdiere, S.S.S., Ph.D., S.T.L.
Peg Bowman, M.A.
Gerald Darring, M.A.
Brian DuSell, D.M.A.
Teresa DuSell, M.M.
Bryan T. Froehle, Ph.D.
Thomas J. McGrath
Joanne Paprocki, M.A.
Daniel L. Snyder, M.Div., Ph.D.
Christopher R. Weickert
Elaine M. Weickert

Catechetical Staff

Jeanette L. Graham, M.A.
Marlene Halpin, O.P., Ph.D.
Thomas McLaughlin, M.A.
Joseph Paprocki, M.A.

Grateful acknowledgment is given to authors, publishers, photographers, museums, and agents for permission to reprint the following copyrighted material; music credits where appropriate can be found at the bottom of each individual song. Every effort has been made to determine copyright owners. In the case of any omissions, the publisher will be pleased to make suitable acknowledgments in future editions. Continued on page 335.

Cover Design: Think Design Group
Cover Illustration: Christina Balit
Interior Design: Three Communication Design

ISBN-13: 978-0-8294-1821-7
ISBN-10: 0-8294-1821-0

Manufactured in the United States of America.

LOYOLA PRESS.
A JESUIT MINISTRY

3441 N. Ashland Avenue
Chicago, Illinois 60657
(800) 621-1008
www.loyolapress.com

RRD / Menasha, WI USA / 02-10 / 4th printing

Table of Contents

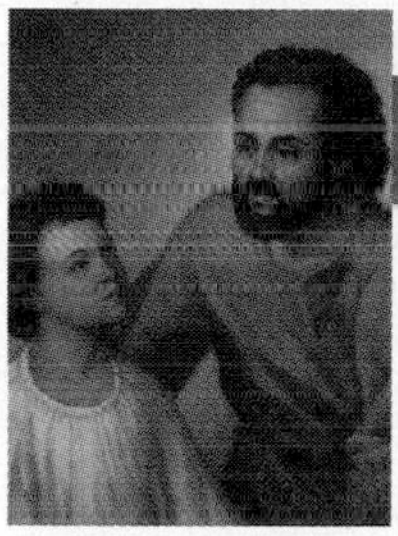

God Loves Us

Unit 1

Saint Francis of Assisi

Saint Francis loved all living things.

Saint Francis

Francis liked the country. He loved the trees. He loved the animals.

Once a hungry wolf began to bother people. The people were scared.

Francis was not. He talked to "brother wolf." He gave the wolf food. Soon, no one was scared. "Brother wolf" was their friend.

God Made Everything

Session 1

Think about the wonderful world around you. Think about the animals. Think about the trees and the flowers. Think about your friends and your family.

What are your favorite things?

Prayer

God, help me see the beauty of your world.
Help me always know that you love me.

God Is the Creator

God is the **creator** of everything. God made the sky and the sea. God made trees and flowers. He even made us.

God loves us. He wants us to enjoy all he made.

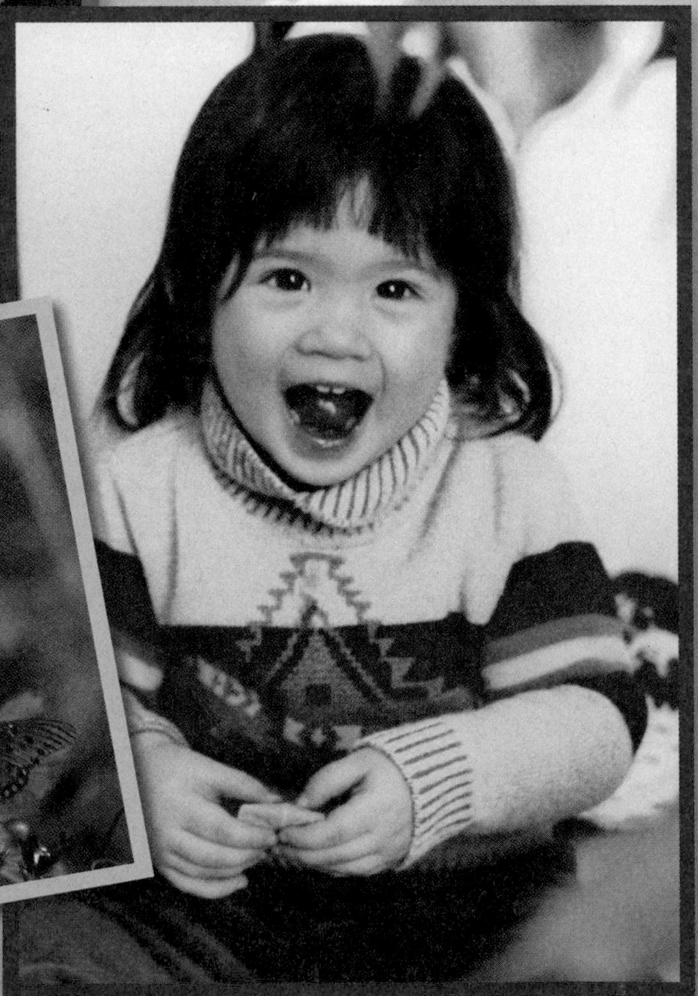

God Makes Good Things

God looked at everything he made. He saw green plants, sweet fruit, and fresh water. He said, "It is very good."

adapted from Genesis 1:31

Think about crunchy lettuce, sweet apples, and pretty birds. Draw your favorite things God made.

Reading God's Word

Clouds play in the sky. Flowers bloom on earth. Trees bow their branches to God. All are happy. God is good.

adapted from Psalm 96:11-13

Take Care of Our World

God wants us to be happy. How? We can love God and others. We can work together. We can play with one another. We can take care of our world.

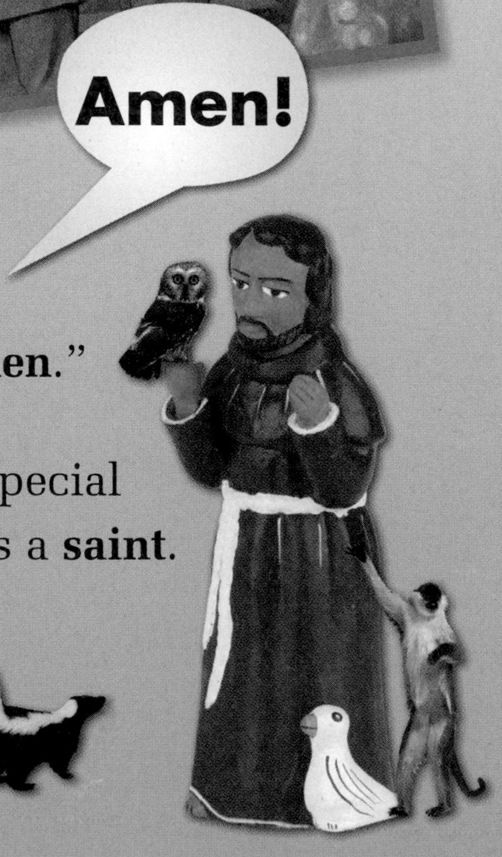

We can show love for God by praying. When we have finished, we pray "**Amen**."

Some people show love for God in a special way. Francis of Assisi did this. He was a **saint**.

Helping Others

People show love for God's world by helping others.

Some people build homes. ▶

▲ Some people share their food and clothes.

Meet a Saint

Saint Vincent de Paul lived long ago.
He helped people who were poor and in need.
This is how he showed God his love.

Prayer

When we pray, we talk to God. We think of him. We ask him for what we need. We begin and end our prayer with the Sign of the Cross.

In the name of the Father,

and of the Son,

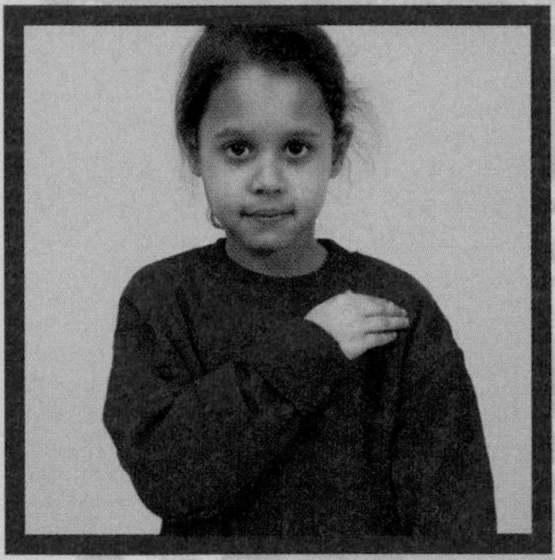

and of the Holy

Spirit.

Amen.

Show God your love. Talk with God in your heart. Tell him what you are thankful for.

Living My Faith

Faith Summary

God is the creator of all people and all things. When we care for the world, we show God our love.

Words I Learned

Amen **creator** **God** **saint**

Ways of Being Like Jesus

Show that you love God's world. Put trash where it belongs.

With My Family

Tell your family what you like about them. Tell them, "Mom, I like your singing. Dad, I like your cooking."

Prayer

Thank you, God, for making this great world for us.

My Response

How can you show that you love God's world?

Focus on Faith

God Made Everything Good

A father was looking at his two-year-old son. Never had he imagined the joy that having a child would bring to his life. Until this point, he had not given much thought to God; in fact, he was not even sure that he believed in God. On this day, however, he noticed his little boy's perfectly shaped ear. It must have been formed deliberately and intricately to perform its function of gathering sound. The father marveled at how something so seemingly ordinary as an ear could be formed so flawlessly. Amid these thoughts, he realized that he was looking directly at the wonder of creation. He saw how good it was. At that moment, he realized that his son existed because of something much larger than he: a loving, caring God.

The Creation of the Animals (detail), Grabow Altarpiece, Bertram

Dinnertime Conversation Starter

Think about the wonders of creation that you noticed today. Consider the most minute to the most grand. Share these with your child, while encouraging him or her to do the same.

Spirituality in Action

Go on a nature walk with your child to instill in him or her an appreciation for God's world. Point out the beauty that surrounds you: trees, grass, flowers, birds, insects, smells, and sounds. Explain to your child that God made all these wonderful things for us to enjoy. Talk about how you can show respect for nature and care for it.

Hints for at Home

Plant flower or vegetable seeds in small paper cups. As a family, talk about how God created everything—from flowers to oceans to people. All of God's creation is precious and special in its own way, and we can each show our appreciation by caring for it. Discuss with your child simple ways in which he or she can care for God's world. When the plants grow large enough, encourage your child to give them away as gifts or plant them in your neighborhood.

Focus on Prayer

Your child has learned that when we pray, we open our minds and hearts to God and ask him for the things we need. Practice beginning and ending prayer with the Sign of the Cross.

God Cares for Us

Session 2

Were you ever new to a group? Were you scared? Did someone help you feel welcome? How?

Prayer

Loving God, teach me to care for others.
Help me show your love to others.

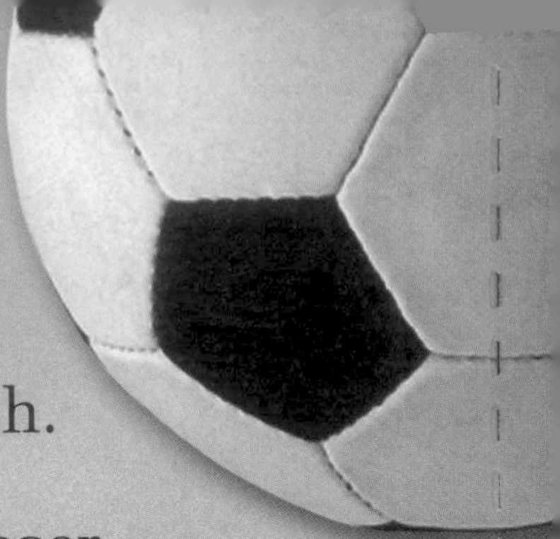

Showing God's Love

A new boy came to school. His name is Lee. He seemed shy. He did not speak much English.

At recess he sat alone. He watched us play soccer. He watched every move.

Yesterday I asked Lee to play with us. He jumped up and smiled. "OK!" he said.

Lee is the best soccer player of us all! He teaches me new moves. I teach him words in English. I am glad to have my new friend, Lee.

God loves us and cares for us. That is why he made us. He made us to be like him. We are like God when we love and care for others.

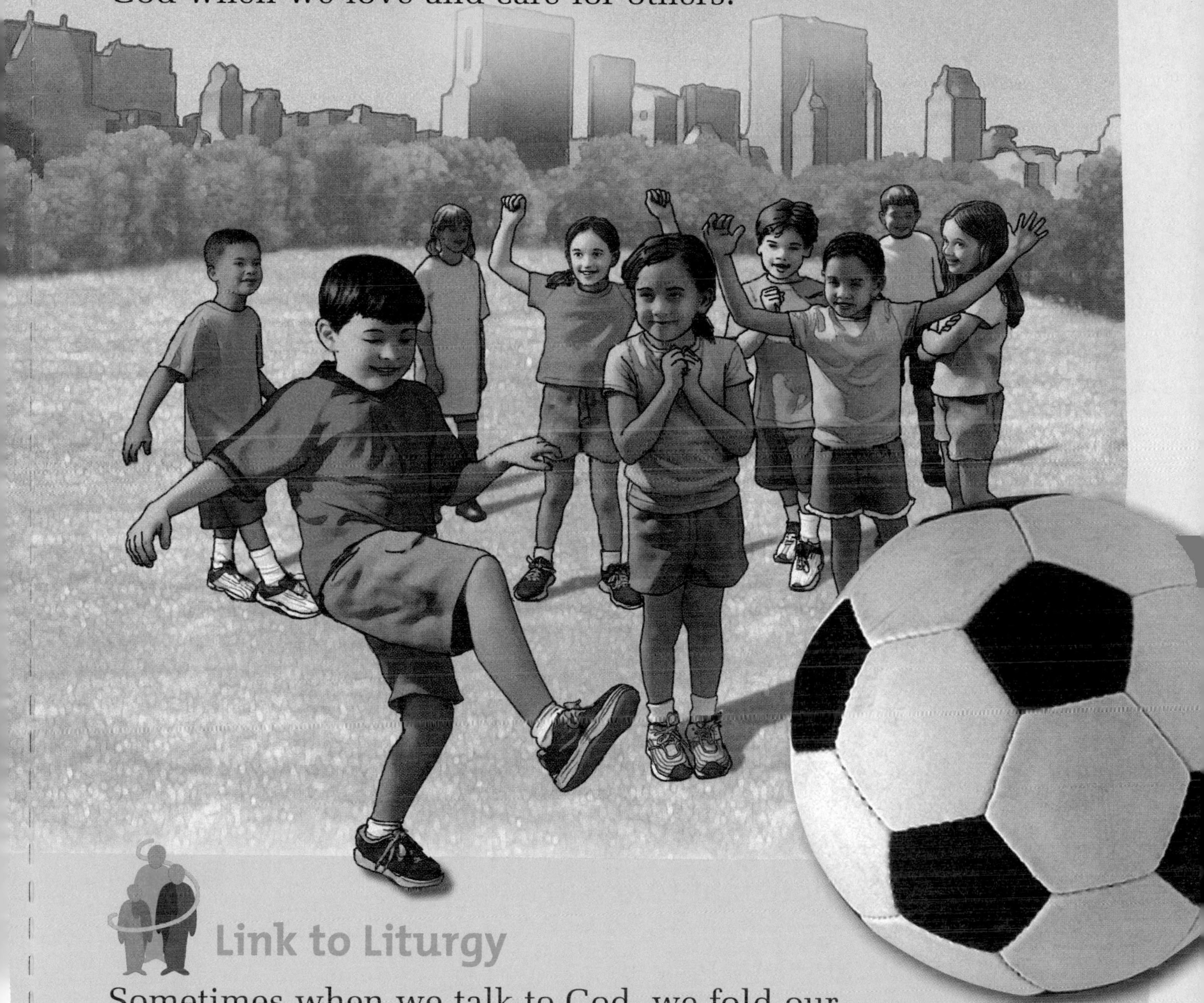

Link to Liturgy

Sometimes when we talk to God, we fold our hands. We raise our hearts and minds to God.

God's Perfect World

God said, "I give you all the plants and trees.
They have seeds and fruit for you to eat."

adapted from Genesis 1:29

How do we know that God cares for us?

He gives us good things.

Name the good things in the picture.
Then color the children.

Showing God We Care

Together at **Mass** we hear stories about God.
We pray together. We sing together.
We show our love for God.
Mass is a special kind of **liturgy**.

Reading God's Word

I will enjoy the good things God has given me.

adapted from Psalm 27:13

Prayer

We give thanks to God with special words. These are words that you can pray.

We praise you.
We bless you.
We thank you.

God loves and cares for you. You are so special!

In your heart, talk with God. Thank him for the way he cares for you.

Living My Faith

Faith Summary

God loves us. He loves us more than anyone else can. God wants us to love one another.

Words I Learned

liturgy **Mass**

Ways of Being Like Jesus

Show others you care. Say hello to students you do not know. Play with them at recess.

With My Family

Show your family you love them. Can you sweep the floor? Can you water the plants?

Prayer

Thank you, God, for loving me and caring for me.

My Response

God cares for us. How can you care for others?

Focus on Faith

God Created Us Because He Loves Us

When you walk into your child's bedroom, what do you see? What is it that makes the room unique? Perhaps you see the quilt that was specially made by Grandma. Maybe pictures of sports or cartoon heroes adorn a wall. Books on dinosaurs or other favorite animals may fill bookcases. Drawings of dragons or butterflies may decorate the room. Think for a moment how much you can learn about your child by noticing the things collected and loved by him or her. In much the same way, we receive a reflection of who God is through the things present in his world. When we look thoughtfully at the world he created and when we note the things with which he surrounds us, we truly discover his love and caring for us.

Dinnertime Conversation Starter

Talk about something you saw today that reminded you of your child. Then ask family members to take turns sharing their impressions of things they saw that reminded them of God. Point out how these things demonstrate his love for us.

In Our Parish

Your child is beginning to learn the meaning of the Mass as liturgy. Guide your child to fold his or her hands at the appropriate times during Mass, and be sure to compliment your child when this is done correctly.

Spirituality in Action

We serve God when we serve others. Talk to your child about ways he or she can care for others. Tell your child how your parish community helps others, whether it be through food drives, bake sales, or volunteer work. Additionally, the Family Cares organization is an excellent resource for families that are interested in learning how they can change the world around them through charity work. Through simple and engaging projects, activities, and volunteer work, Family Cares offers numerous practical ideas to parents for developing a sense of charity and goodwill in their children. Visit the organization at **www.familycares.org.**

Focus on Prayer

Your child is learning how to fold his or her hands, a gesture that shows honor and love for God while praying. This gesture also shows that we belong to Jesus. Fold hands with your child while reflecting silently. Be sure to pray the Sign of the Cross together at the beginning and end of prayer time.

God Is Our Father

Session

3

Whose birthday is it? How is the family showing love?

Think of your family.
How can you show your love?

Prayer

God, help me learn about your love.
Help me grow closer to you.

A Special Message

Today is Ben's birthday.
His father gives him a special card.

DEAR BEN,
YOU ARE VERY SPECIAL TO ME.
YOU ARE KIND TO OUR FAMILY.
I WILL LOVE YOU ALWAYS.
- DAD

Did you ever get a special message?
How did it make you feel?

God's Message

God our Father sends us a message. He loves and cares for us. God's message is in the **Bible.** The Bible also tells us about **Jesus**, God's son.

Link to Liturgy

At Mass we hear stories from the Bible.

God Gave Us His Son

God wants us to know about him. He sent his Son, Jesus, to us. Jesus teaches us that God is our Father. Jesus tells us how much God loves us.

God said, "This is my wonderful Son. I love him so. He makes me happy with everything he does."

adapted from Matthew 3:17

A Home With Jesus

Imagine Jesus is coming to your home. How do you greet him? Who else is there to welcome him? What do you do when he comes?

Draw a picture of Jesus in your home.

Reading God's Word

Jesus said, "If you love me, my Father will love you. We will live with you in love."

adapted from John 14:23

Prayer

Imagine Jesus is speaking to you telling you how special you are! He tells you how much God loves you. He tells you this is God's message in the Bible.

Meet Jesus in your heart. Talk with him. Know that he hears your words. Be still with Jesus.

Living My Faith

Faith Summary

God our Father and his Son, Jesus, speak to us in a special way. We learn about God's love in the Bible.

Words I Learned

Bible **Jesus**

Ways of Being Like Jesus

Share God's message.
Say, "God loves you."
Say, "I love you too."

With My Family

Put your family Bible in a special place. Ask your mom or dad to read with you.

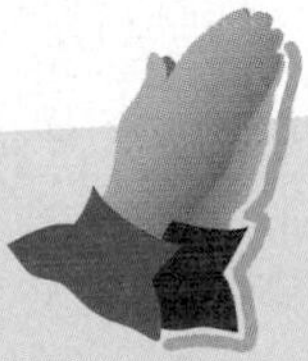

Prayer

Thank you, God, for your message in the Bible.

My Response

Think of God's message to you. What can you do to show you hear his message?

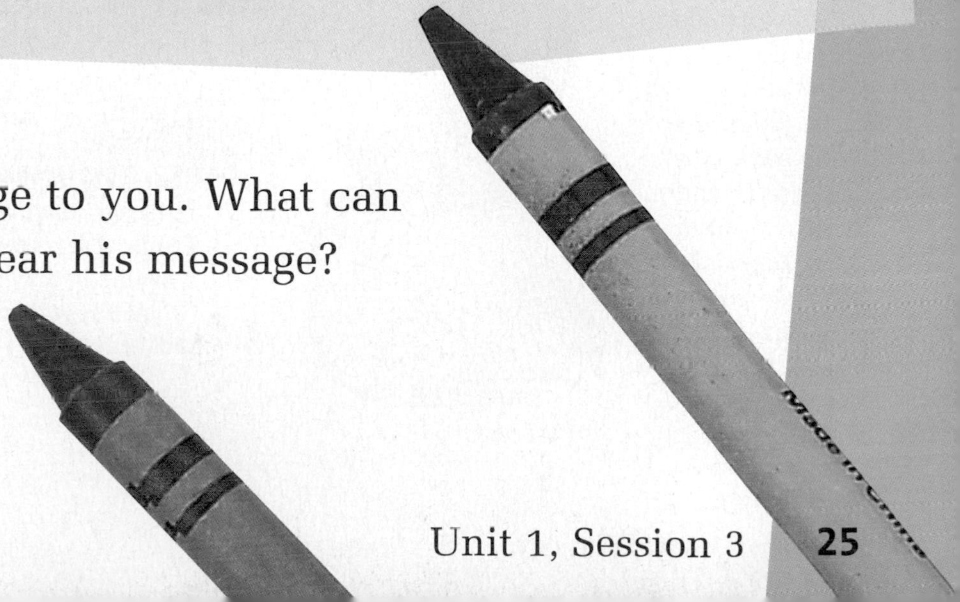

Focus on Faith

God, Our Loving Father

What a wonderful foster father Joseph was to Jesus. From the time Jesus was born, Joseph cared deeply for Jesus, protecting him, loving him, and teaching him. In return Jesus had the greatest respect for Joseph.

It can be a little frightening and overwhelming to know that we are our children's primary teachers in life. The family environment is where fundamental values are first formed and where children are taught what it means to be a loving parent. What children learn in the home will heavily influence how they respond when hearing that Jesus tells us to refer to God as Father.

Dinnertime Conversation Starter

Share with other members of your family something you have learned from each of them. Ask them to do the same. This is a great opportunity to observe how your child interprets your words and actions.

Our Catholic Heritage

Many people of many backgrounds contributed to the writing of the Bible, which occurred over a span of about 1,500 years. It remains the best-selling book in history.

Hints for at Home

Create a Prayer Rock. Help your child look for a special rock. Wrap the rock in soft fabric and attach a copy of the poem below while discussing the importance of prayer. Have your child place the fabric-covered rock on his or her pillow, where it will serve as a reminder to think about God each night before bedtime.

I'm a little prayer rock,
And this is what I'll do:
Put me on your pillow,
Until the day is through.
Then turn back the covers,
Climb into bed with care,
And you will find your prayer rock sitting right there.
You will then remember
To fold your hands in prayer.
Ask that God will bless you,
And keep you in God's care.

Author Unknown

Focus on Prayer

Your child is making a home for Jesus in his or her heart. Encourage prayer by lighting a candle or playing soft music. Sit quietly with your child and talk to Jesus in your hearts.

God Gives Us Peace Session 4

Think about your friends.
How do you feel when you play together?

Prayer

God, help me live in peace.
I want to share your peace with others.

A Gift of Peace

Jesus' friends were in a room. Jesus came to see them. He said, "Peace be with you. My Father sent me to you. Now I send you to help others." He breathed on them. Then he said, "The **Holy Spirit** is with you."

adapted from John 20:19-22

Jesus gives us the Holy Spirit.
The Holy Spirit is always with us.
He brings us God's peace.

How Can You Bring Peace?

You can pray for peace. You can even play for peace! Children play for peace all over the world. First one child laughs. Then another child laughs. Soon, everyone laughs together. Peace is everywhere!

Reading God's Word

Peace and love be to you from God the Father and his Son, Jesus.

adapted from Ephesians 6:23

All Are One

The Father, the Son, and the Holy Spirit are the **Trinity**.

God our Father made us.

Jesus his Son brings us God's love.

The Holy Spirit brings us peace.

God made us out of love. Love and peace are God's gifts to us.

Father, Son, and Holy Spirit

What do we call the Father, the Son, and the Holy Spirit? Find the word. Color the spaces that have dots.

Did You Know?

When you see a friend, what do you say? When Saint Francis saw a friend, he said something special. He said, "Peace and goodness." Try it!

Peace and goodness.

Prayer

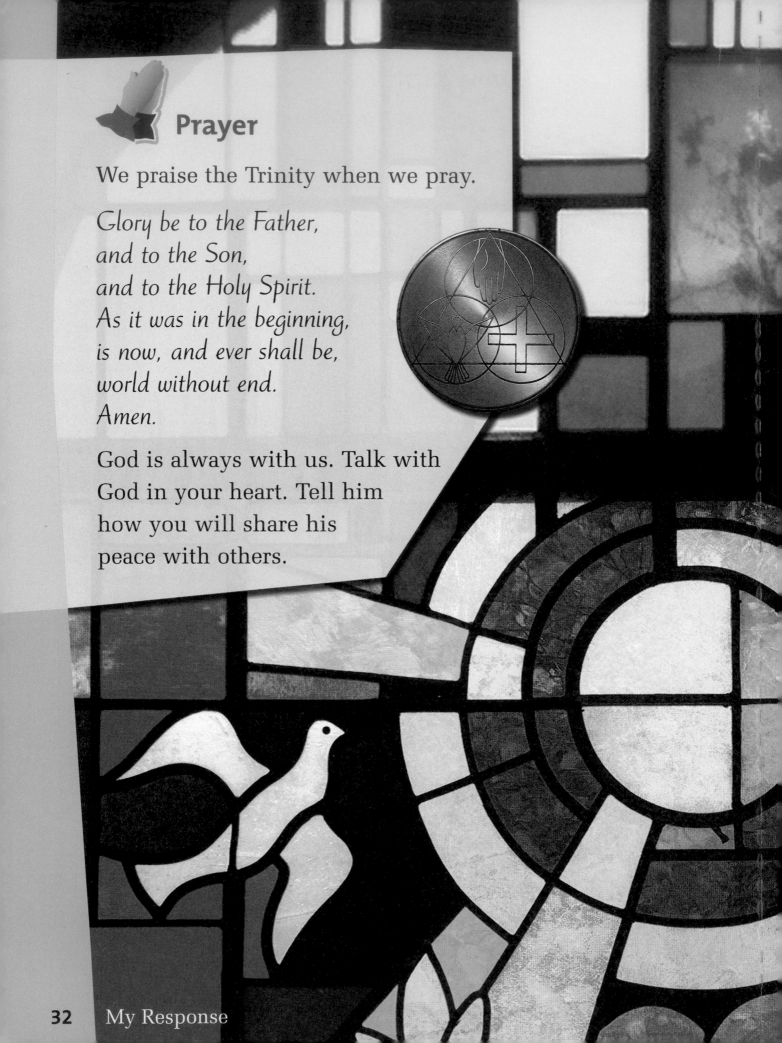

We praise the Trinity when we pray.

Glory be to the Father,
and to the Son,
and to the Holy Spirit.
As it was in the beginning,
is now, and ever shall be,
world without end.
Amen.

God is always with us. Talk with God in your heart. Tell him how you will share his peace with others.

Living My Faith

Faith Summary

God is always with us. God the Father made us. Jesus his Son brings us the Father's love. The Holy Spirit brings us peace.

Words I Learned

Holy Spirit **Trinity**

Ways of Being Like Jesus

Jesus brings us God's love.
You can bring God's love.
You can share your toys.

With My Family

Talk with your family at dinner.
Take turns talking about your day.

Prayer

Thank you, Jesus, for bringing peace to my life.

My Response

How can you bring peace to someone who is upset?

RAISING FAITH-FILLED KIDS
a parent page

Focus on Faith

The Holy Spirit Helps Us Feel Loved

Everyone needs approval. Feeling appreciated and liked is especially important in the life of a child. Our words are extremely powerful, because they help to form our children's identities. When we think about this issue, it is helpful to remember and reflect on the people in our lives who helped us to realize how important we are. Our hearts can skip a beat just thinking of their words of approval. This sense of well-being is one of the ways we recognize the depth of God's love for us. As our children come before us in fragility and hope, we must recognize the opportunity presented to us: discovering the individuals whom the Holy Spirit is calling our children to be. What could be more valuable?

Dinnertime Conversation Starter

Share with your child something you recall about a person who was important to you. What did this person say or do that made such an impression? Talk together about people who are important in your child's life. Are there similarities?

Our Catholic Heritage

Many people work hard for peace. During the Great Depression, Dorothy Day formed the Catholic Worker Movement and dedicated her life to providing food, clothing, and shelter to people who were poor, while fighting passionately for peace and equality. She believed so strongly in her cause that she voluntarily led a life of poverty. Today, she is remembered as a holy person.

Spirituality in Action

One of the most important things you can do as a parent to instill a sense of peace in your child is to demonstrate your own respect for people of different cultures, ethnicities, and religions. Go to your local library with your child to find books that show peaceful living. One fun book that encourages peace by highlighting similarities in children around the globe is *All in a Day* by Mitsumasa Anno and other authors.

Focus on Prayer

Your child is learning to celebrate God as Father, Son, and Holy Spirit through the prayer Glory Be to the Father. The more often the prayer is prayed in the home, the quicker and easier it will be for your child to memorize it. Have your family take turns leading the prayer. Visit www.FindingGod.org for words to the prayer.

Review

Session 5

This church honors Saint Francis of Assisi.
He loved and cared for everything God made.

Prayer

God, help me take care of your world.
I want to show you my love for everything you created.

Faith Summary

God is our Father and Creator. He loves us more than anyone else loves us.

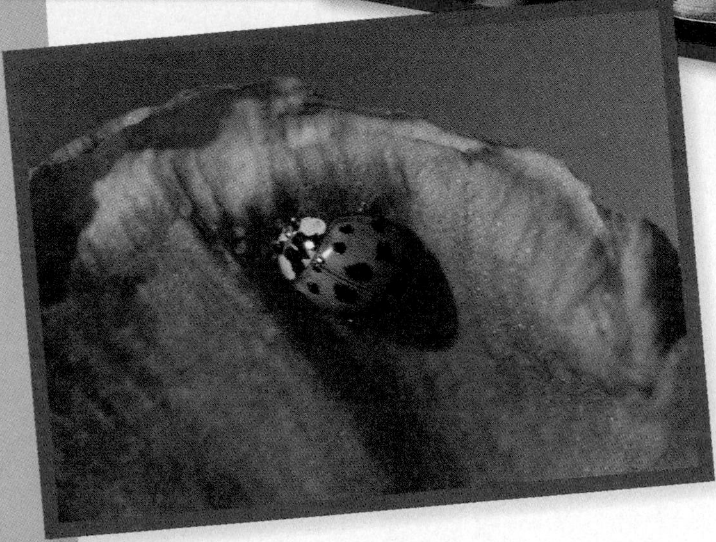

God wants us to know him. He sent us his Son, Jesus. God also gave us the Bible.

God is always near. The Father, Son, and Holy Spirit are the Trinity.

Saint Francis and His Friends

Cut out the pictures. Tell a story.

Prayer Service

Leader: *Praise be to God, for he made this wonderful world and everything in it.*

All: *Amen.*

Leader: *A reading from the book of Genesis.*

Then God said, "Let there be light," and there was light.

[Genesis 1:3]

The Word of the Lord.

All: *Thanks be to God.*

Leader: *God's love is all around you.*
God will always care for you.
Let us pray together.

All: *Glory be to the Father,*
and to the Son,
and to the Holy Spirit.
As it was in the beginning,
is now, and ever shall be,
world without end.
Amen.

Living My Faith

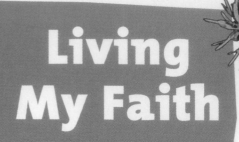

Ways of Being Like Jesus

Bring Jesus' message of love and peace to others. Invite a new friend to your house to play. Help someone without being asked.

With My Family

Help keep your home beautiful. Ask your parents for some seeds. Plant a little garden. Take good care of it.

Prayer

Thank you, God, for giving me your world.
Thank you for your love and peace.
Thank you for caring for me.

My Response

How can you show your love for God?

Jesus Loves Us

Unit
2

Saint Joseph

Saint Joseph was Jesus' foster father.
He was a good man, and he loved God.

Saint Joseph

Joseph was a carpenter.
He worked hard.

Mary was Joseph's wife.
She was going to have a baby.

An angel spoke to Joseph. The angel said that Mary's baby would be called Jesus.

Joseph cared for Jesus and Mary his whole life.

God Sends Jesus

Session

6

David has a new sister.

Katie has a new puppy.

What is new in your family?

How does having something new make you feel?

Prayer

Loving God, show me how to always welcome Jesus into my heart.

Jesus Is Born

Mary was going to have a baby. She and **Joseph** were far from home. There was no room for them at the inn. Imagine how they felt.

Mary and Joseph stayed in a stable. This is where Jesus was born. He was the Son of God.

It was a special time when Jesus was born. Shepherds were in the fields. God sent **angels** to them. The angels sang songs. They told the shepherds where to find Jesus.

adapted from Luke 2:4-14

Did You Know?

The name *Jesus* means "God saves." God sent Jesus to save us.

Shepherds Visit Jesus

The shepherds were the first to see Jesus. They were people like you and me. This is how God wanted it. We celebrate Jesus' birth at **Christmas**.

Reading God's Word

Mary kept her feelings in her heart. The shepherds thanked God for all they heard and saw.

adapted from Luke 2:19-20

Born in a Stable

Jesus is the Son of God, who became man.
Jesus was born in a stable. Why?
God wanted to teach us something.
We can find him in unexpected places.

The Holy Family

God sent us his only Son, Jesus.
Joseph and Mary cared for him.
We call Jesus, Mary, and Joseph
the **Holy Family**.

Who's Who?

Look at the pictures below.
Write the name of each person
on the line.

Prayer

Imagine you are with the Holy Family. You are in the stable where Jesus was born.

Look around. What is it like? Ask Mary and Joseph if you may hold their new baby.

Jesus is in your arms. You hold him against your heart. What do you want to say to him? Let him know how much you love him. Then give him back to Mary and Joseph.

Living My Faith

Faith Summary

God wanted to show us his love. He sent us his Son, Jesus. Joseph and Mary were Jesus' parents on earth. Jesus needed them both.

Words I Learned

angel **Christmas** **Holy Family**

Joseph **Mary**

Ways of Being Like Jesus

Be friendly to someone you just met.

With My Family

Ask your family about the day you were born. What was it like?

Prayer

Thank you, God, for sending us Jesus.

My Response

How can you welcome Jesus into your heart?

Focus on Faith

Jesus Is Born

The commercial hype surrounding Christmas seems to come earlier every year. The sentimental music, redundant decorations, and blatant consumerism leave us exhausted. Who can really celebrate anything in the middle of all the noise? The true story of Jesus' birth is quite simple: it tells us that when we look for God, we will find him in unexpected places. When God the Father sent Jesus, he chose a humble stable to be the birthplace. For Jesus' parents, God chose Mary and Joseph—good, modest people who loved and cared for Jesus. He selected poor shepherds to be the first to learn of the coming of Jesus. At its heart, the Christmas story calls us to focus on God's presence all around us and examine what is truly important in our lives. We can prepare for Christmas with planned moments of peace.

Dinnertime Conversation Starter

Begin a discussion about how you will celebrate the holiday season in your home. How will you remember the birth of Jesus?

The Nativity, Gustave Doré

Spirituality in Action

Talk with your child about how God especially blesses those in need. Encourage small acts of generosity, such as opening doors for others, giving up a seat on a bus, and carrying someone's groceries.

Hints for at Home

Build a manger. With your child, gather twigs, leaves, and dried grass. At home, create a support by fastening the twigs together with twine or glue. Then arrange the remaining twigs across the support and add grass and leaves. Keep your manger until Advent, and place it on a mantle or under the Christmas tree to remind you why this time is special.

Focus on Prayer

Your child is learning to pray with the Holy Family. Ask him or her to tell you why Jesus, Mary, and Joseph are special. Then light a candle, and pray silently with your child.

Jesus Teaches Us

Session 7

On the way home Eddie fell asleep in the car. Dad carried him into the house and to his room.

When did someone take care of you? What did he or she do for you? How did you feel?

Prayer

Caring Jesus, guide me when I talk to God.
I want to be close to him.

Jesus Prayed to God

Jesus talked to and listened to God. Jesus gave us a special **prayer.** It is called the Lord's Prayer. When we pray it, we grow closer to God, Jesus, and one another.

Reading God's Word

Jesus went up the mountain to pray.
All night long he prayed to God.

adapted from Luke 6:12

The Lord's Prayer

The Lord's Prayer is very important. Listen for it at Mass. It starts like this:

Our Father,	God is our Father.
who art in heaven,	Heaven is life with God.
hallowed be thy name;	God's name is holy.
thy kingdom *come;*	God's way becomes our way.
thy will be done	We ask God to guide us.
on earth as it is in heaven.	We pray that people will do what is pleasing to God.

adapted from Matthew 6:9-10

Being Kind to Others

Eve's parents work hard. She wants to do something kind for them.

Eve did a good thing. She helped serve the **Kingdom of God**.

Did You Know?

Long ago pretzels were given to children who learned their prayers. Can you see why?

God's Kingdom

How can you serve the Kingdom of God?
Put an **X** in the box.

Prayer

Jesus taught us a special prayer.

Our Father,
who art in heaven,
hallowed be thy name;
thy kingdom come;
thy will be done
on earth as it is in heaven.

Talk to Jesus in your heart. Thank him for teaching you how to pray. Tell him you will talk with God, as he did.

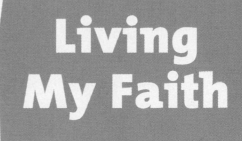

Living My Faith

Faith Summary

Jesus taught us the Lord's Prayer. It is our most important prayer.

Words I Learned

heaven **Kingdom of God** **prayer**

Ways of Being Like Jesus

Jesus taught his friends how to pray. You are his friend. Ask him to help you pray.

With My Family

Pray with your family before bedtime.

Prayer

Thank you, Jesus, for teaching me how to pray.
I will talk to God every day.

My Response

What can you do at school to serve the Kingdom of God?

Focus on Faith

Speaking to Our Father

It was not so long ago that you first heard your child say, "Mama" or "Dada." That first sign of recognition of the relationship we have with our children will always be a treasure. Even today, when we see our children after school, we experience a personal thrill and comfort in hearing them call, "Hi, Mom" or "Hi, Dad." Joseph must have felt a similar thrill when Jesus called him *Abba,* the Hebrew word for "Dad." We know that Jesus had a special affection for the word, because when his disciples asked him how to pray, he told them to address God as *Abba.* Jesus teaches us to recognize that, just as we are thrilled to hear from our children, God our Father is always happy to hear from us.

Dinnertime Conversation Starter

Jesus referred to God as *Abba,* or Dad. Tell the story of your name. Were you named after someone? If so, after whom? What is the meaning of your name? Do you have a nickname? Discuss how each family member came to be named.

Spirituality in Action

In God's eyes we are all brothers and sisters. Children learn from their parents how to treat others. Talk with your child about how God wants us to treat others. Discuss ways to be friendly to a new student. Encourage ideas about sharing toys, playing fairly, and including others.

Hints for at Home

Make a Lord's Prayer Jigsaw Puzzle. On a large piece of paper or poster board, print the first half of the Lord's Prayer, separating it into short phrases. Let your child color or paint the background. Then, carefully cut out each phrase, altering the shapes slightly so that they resemble puzzle pieces. Now, let your child put the prayer back together.

Focus on Prayer

Your child is learning the first half of the Lord's Prayer. Pray it together slowly and clearly to help him or her memorize and understand it. Visit www.FindingGod.org for the words to the Lord's Prayer.

Trust in God

Session
8

If you had one wish, what would you wish for?

Is this something you really need?

What about a big hug when you are sad?

What about laughter with a friend?

Prayer

Jesus, my friend, help me trust God in all things.

The Lord's Prayer

We learned how the Lord's Prayer begins.

Our Father,
who art in heaven,
hallowed be thy name;
thy kingdom come;
thy will be done
on earth as it is in heaven.

Now we will learn the rest.

Give us this day our daily bread;	We ask God to give us what we need.
*and forgive us our **trespasses***	We ask God to forgive us for hurting others.

as we forgive those who trespass against us;	We ask God to help us forgive those who have hurt us.
and lead us not into ***temptation,***	We ask God to help us to make good decisions.
but deliver us from evil.	We ask God to protect us.
Amen.	We say yes to God.

adapted from Matthew 6:11-13

Link to Liturgy

We always pray the Lord's Prayer at Mass. Sometimes we sing it. Sometimes we speak it.

Saying We Are Sorry

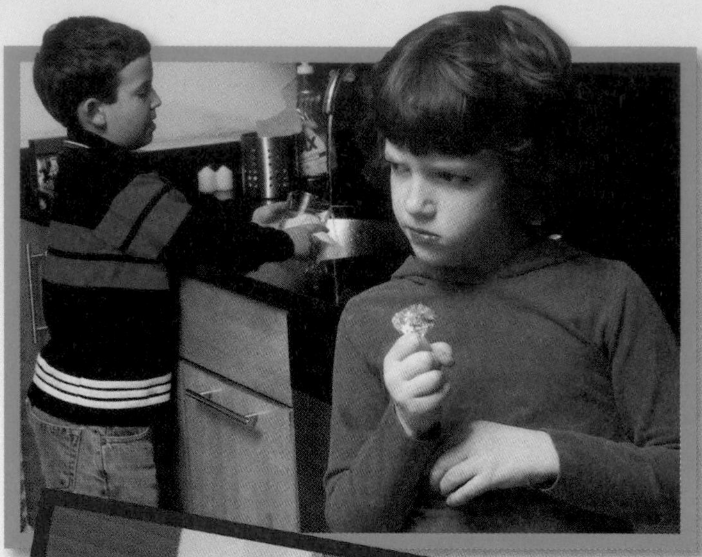

Meg's brother, Brad, had candy. Meg wanted it very much. So she took it.

Brad was upset. Meg felt bad. She thought about what she had done.

Meg knew what to do. She told Brad, "I am sorry."

Brad smiled and said, "OK."

Meg said, "Do you want to play my new game?" They played together happily.

Needs or Wants?

God wants us to have everything we need.
What do you really need? Draw circles.

Reading God's Word

God is happy to give you his kingdom.

adapted from Luke 12:32

Prayer

The Lord's Prayer helps us tell God what we need.

Our Father,
who art in heaven,
hallowed be thy name;
thy kingdom come;
thy will be done
on earth as it is in heaven.
Give us this day our daily bread;
and forgive us our trespasses
as we forgive those
who trespass against us;
and lead us not into temptation,
but deliver us from evil.
Amen.

Think about what you just asked God to do for you. Thank him for giving you what you need.

Living My Faith

Faith Summary

In the Lord's Prayer we ask God to give us what we need. We ask him to protect us. We ask him to forgive us and to help us forgive others.

Words I Learned

temptation **trespasses**

Ways of Being Like Jesus

Ask God for only what you truly need. This is what Jesus did.

With My Family

Give your family something they need. Give Mom or Dad a big hug for no reason.

Prayer

Thank you, God, for giving me what I need.

My Response

We trust God to give us what we need. How can you show that you can be trusted?

RAISING FAITH-FILLED KIDS

a parent page

Focus on Faith

Our Daily Bread

As parents, we want to give our children everything they need. We want them to have a secure home to keep them safe, a balanced diet to keep them healthy, and the clothes they need to protect them from the elements. When we pray the Lord's Prayer and ask God for our daily bread, we are asking him to give us what we need. When we satisfy our children's needs, we are fulfilling their prayers, for it is through us that God answers them.

Dinnertime Conversation Starter

Discuss with your family the difference between needs and wants. How can personal wants interfere with the needs of others?

Hints for at Home

Talk with your child about one simple need each member of your family has. How can you give each person what he or she needs? For example, for a family member who needs time to rest, make a Quiet Time sign to hang on a doorknob. Color it and decorate it with yarn.

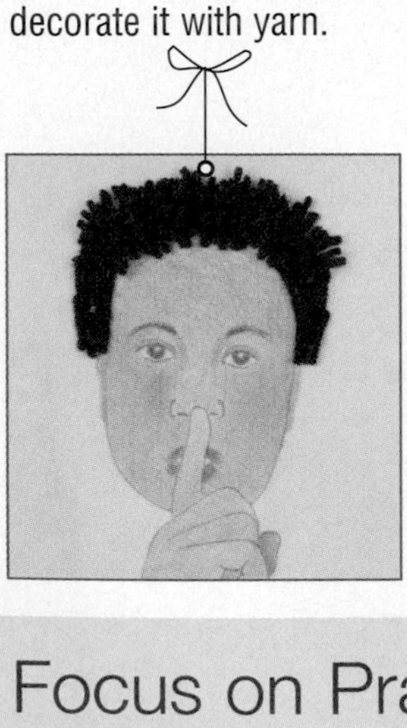

Spirituality in Action

With your child, set aside some time to gather clean clothing you no longer need. Collect coats, shoes, hats, pants, and shirts in good condition. As you do this, talk with him or her about the difference between needs and wants, and discuss additional ways of filling the needs of others. Then donate the clothing to your parish or your local thrift store.

Focus on Prayer

Your child has completed learning the Lord's Prayer. Pray the prayer together slowly and clearly; make sure your child understands the words and their meanings. Visit **www.FindingGod.org** for the words to the Lord's Prayer.

Jesus Rises From the Dead

Session 9

Amy could not find her puppy.
She looked upstairs.
She looked downstairs.
Amy looked all morning.
Tears rolled down her face.

Then she heard a bark at the door.
Amy was so happy!

Did you ever find something
that you had lost?
How did you feel?

Prayer

Dear Jesus, help me remember you are always with me.

Jesus Is Risen

When Jesus died, his friends were sad. They missed him a lot. Two women went to his tomb. An angel was there. The women were scared.

The angel said, "Do not be afraid. I know you are looking for Jesus. You think he is dead, but he is not. Jesus **Christ** is alive! Go tell your friends."

The women were full of joy! They ran to tell their friends.

On the way they saw Jesus. He was walking on the road.

They were so happy! They cried with joy. He said, "Do not be afraid. Tell my friends to go into town. I will see them there."

adapted from Matthew 28:1-10

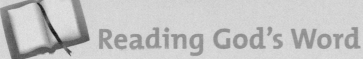

Reading God's Word

Whenever people come together for me, I am with them.

adapted from Matthew 18:20

Jesus Is Alive!

Jesus rose from the dead. We call this the **Resurrection**.

He Is With Us Always

Jesus' friends remembered all he taught them. They knew he was with them when they prayed. Jesus is with us, too, when we pray.

Did You Know?

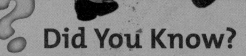

People around the world celebrate Jesus' Resurrection. We call this celebration Easter.

Finding Jesus

Help the women find the tomb.
Then help them find Jesus Christ.

Prayer

Jesus is always with you. He is with you when you think about him. He is with you when you pray.

Meet Jesus in your favorite place. Take time to talk with him. What would you like to say? What does Jesus want you to know?

Take a few moments to enjoy having Jesus so close. Tell him how happy you are that he is with you.

Living My Faith

Faith Summary

When Jesus died, his friends were sad. Then they found out Jesus was alive. They were so happy! They prayed and talked together.

Words I Learned

Christ **Resurrection**

Ways of Being Like Jesus

If you find something that someone lost, look for the owner. Return what you found with a smile.

With My Family

Surprise your parents. Make them a note. Put it on a mirror so they will see it.

Prayer

Jesus, my friend, thank you for always being close to me.

My Response

Jesus is always with you. When might you need to talk to him?

Focus on Faith

Jesus Is Alive in Us

After learning that Jesus had been resurrected, the women left his tomb, overjoyed and eager to share the news with the rest of the disciples. While on their way, they met Jesus, who told them to tell the others that he would meet them in Galilee. In saying this, Jesus meant that if his disciples truly wanted to join him, they should not linger in the past; instead, they should celebrate his new way of being alive in the present. Similarly we, too, should look for daily opportunities to join Jesus. Each day we can seek him in the people we meet and serve. An especially important opportunity presents itself through our growing children: As they grow in their faith and love, they offer us new ways of discovering Jesus' presence in our world.

Dinnertime Conversation Starter

Tell your children to imagine that Jesus is at the dinner table with you tonight. What do you want to tell him or ask him? What do you think he will tell you?

Spirituality in Action

Arrange for a group of children or your child's class to visit an assisted living home. Children can sing songs they learned or bring board games to play with the retirees. Explain to the children that they can bring the joy of God to people who are sick and, perhaps, lonely.

Hints for at Home

Ask your child to think of a happy time you had together. Reminisce about that time. Afterward, point out how sharing these memories made that time come alive again. Explain that this is an important way that Jesus is alive among us. Jesus is present whenever we are gathered in his name and loving one another. Create a collage of happy memories, using photos or drawings.

Focus on Prayer

Your child has learned that when people gather in Jesus Christ's name, he is there with them. Invite your child to pray with you. When you finish, spend a few moments in silence, enjoying the presence of Jesus.

Review

Session
10

Saint Joseph's Table

Long ago, far away, it had not rained for a long time. No plants would grow. There was no food. People were very hungry.

They asked Saint Joseph for help. Soon it began to rain. Plants grew. At last, there was food.

People wanted to thank Saint Joseph. They made a great meal. Everyone shared. People still do this today.

Prayer

Jesus, my teacher, help me always remember how much God loves me.

Faith Summary

God sent his Son to show that he loves us.
God chose Joseph and Mary to care for Jesus.

Jesus taught us the Lord's Prayer. In it we ask God to give us what we need. We ask God to forgive us and to help us forgive others.

When Jesus died, his friends were sad. When they found out he was alive, they were very happy!

Christmas in the Philippines

Some people in the Philippines celebrate Christmas in a special way. They hang stars made of paper.

Some stars have lights inside. The light shines through holes in the stars. The light tells us Jesus is with us.

Christmas Star

Make your own Christmas Star.
Color it and cut it out.
Then hang it up.

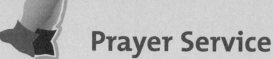

Prayer Service

Leader: *Let us pray the Sign of the Cross.*

Each time we are kind to others, we are giving them something they need.

All: *Jesus, help me to be kind to others.*

Leader: *How we treat those who are less fortunate is how we are treating Jesus.*

All: *Jesus, help me to care for others.*

Leader: *Let us pray the Lord's Prayer.*

All: *Our Father,*
who art in heaven,
hallowed be thy name;
thy kingdom come;
thy will be done
on earth as it is in heaven.
Give us this day our daily bread;
and forgive us our trespasses
as we forgive those
who trespass against us;
and lead us not into temptation,
but deliver us from evil.
Amen.

Living My Faith

Ways of Being Like Jesus

Pray to God the Father often.

With My Family

Do you know anyone who is lonely? Plan a visit or invite him or her to your home.

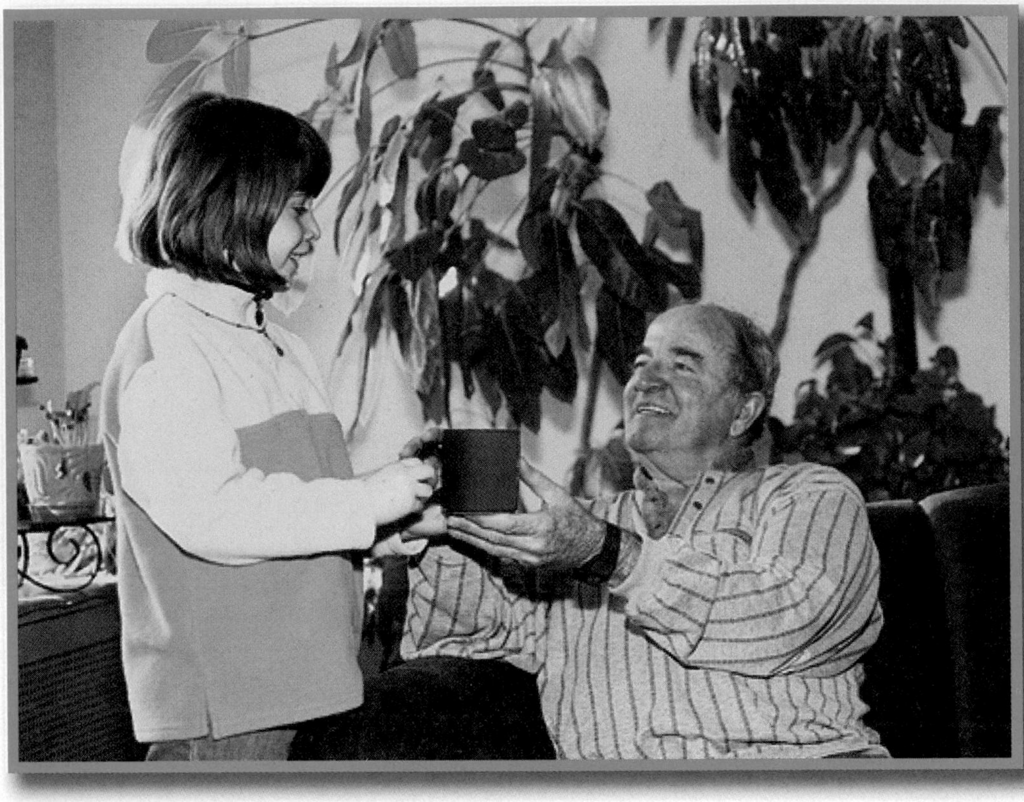

Prayer

Thank you, God, for teaching me to be like Jesus.

My Response

You have learned about Jesus. What was the best thing you learned about him?

All Are Welcome

Unit 3

Saint Peter

Saint Peter was one of Jesus' best friends.

Saint Peter

Long ago there was a fisherman. His name was Peter. Jesus said to him, "Come, follow me." So Peter left his work. He followed Jesus.

Peter loved Jesus. Peter tried to be like Jesus. Sometimes Peter made mistakes. But Jesus always forgave him.

Jesus asked Peter to care for his friends. Peter said yes. So Jesus made Peter the leader of all his people.

Following Jesus

Session
11

Think about a friend of yours. Think about the first time he or she asked you to play. How did you feel?

Prayer

Jesus, my friend, show me how to follow you.
I want to help others.

Jesus Asks Friends to Follow

Peter and his brother, Andrew, were fishermen. One day they were fishing. Jesus passed by. He said to them, “Come, follow me. Learn how to help others. That will be your new work.”

Peter and Andrew left their work. They followed Jesus.

Jesus and his new friends walked. They came to James and his brother, John. They, too, were hard at work.

Jesus spoke to James and John. He asked them to follow him. They left their work to follow Jesus too.

adapted from Mark 1:16-20

Jesus Asks Us to Follow

Long ago Jesus asked these fishermen to follow him. Today he asks us.

Reading God's Word

Follow me. Then you will be my friends.

adapted from John 15:14

Good Friends

Peter, Andrew, James, and John were good friends to Jesus. We need good friends too. Where can we find friends who follow Jesus?

The Church

Today we find Jesus' friends in the **Church**. We follow Jesus together. We learn to love one another. We learn to love others in the world.

Who Is in Your Church?

Jesus' friends are in the Church. Draw them.
Draw yourself too.

Meet a Saint

Saint Michael is a great angel. He cares for police officers. He cares for our Church. You have a special angel caring for you too.

Prayer

Imagine you are playing. You hear someone call your name. You look up. It is Jesus. He asks, "Will you help me? Help me show God's love to others."

Jesus said this to the fishermen. Think about how they trusted Jesus to lead them.

Now spend some time with Jesus. He asks you to help him too. How will you answer Jesus?

Living My Faith

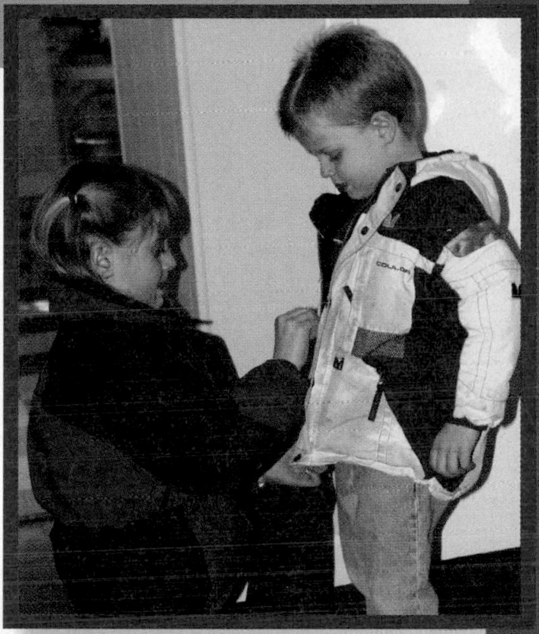

Faith Summary

Jesus gave us the Church.
We find Jesus' friends here.
We learn to love others here.

Word I Learned

Church

Ways of Being Like Jesus

Teach your friends to help people. Set a good example, and be nice to others.

With My Family

Smile when you meet Jesus' friends at church.

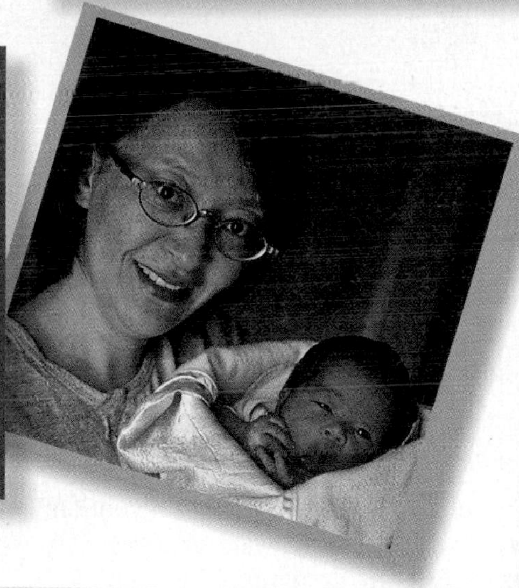

Prayer

Thank you, Jesus, for asking me to help you.

My Response

How can you show your love for Jesus when you are at church?

RAISING FAITH-FILLED KIDS

a parent page

Focus on Faith

We All Need Companions

Each time our children leave our homes, they enter into the real world. Along the way, they make new friends, some of whom become lifelong companions. Jesus knew the importance of having companions. In choosing Peter and the other apostles and disciples, he was taking the first step in establishing the Church. In the Church and especially in our parishes, companions in faith are waiting to walk with our children on their journeys toward God.

Children's greatest influences are their parents. It is through the relationships children form within the family that they learn how to maintain relationships outside the family. By preparing your child now to make friends and to be a friend, you are giving him or her a priceless skill that will be used throughout life.

Dinnertime Conversation Starter

Jesus chose his companions carefully. Ask your child who his or her special friends are. What makes them such good friends? How do they help your child follow Jesus?

Spirituality in Action

With your child, think of ways that your family shows that you are followers of Jesus. Talk about people in your parish who show God's love to others.

Focus on Prayer

Your child is learning to listen to Jesus' call. Discuss what it means to be called by Jesus, and talk about how Jesus calls us through others such as parents and teachers. Light a candle, and spend some moments in silent prayer.

Hints for at Home

Make Friendship Bracelets. You will need assorted beads and craft stems. With your child, arrange the beads on the craft stem, using any color scheme you like. Talk with your child about the importance of friends in our lives. Friends care for us, share with us, teach us, and help us. Have your child give these colorful and uniquely crafted bracelets to people he or she cares about as a reminder of a friendship.

Jesus Sends the Holy Spirit

Session 12

What is a surprise? Did you ever get a wonderful surprise? How did it make you feel?

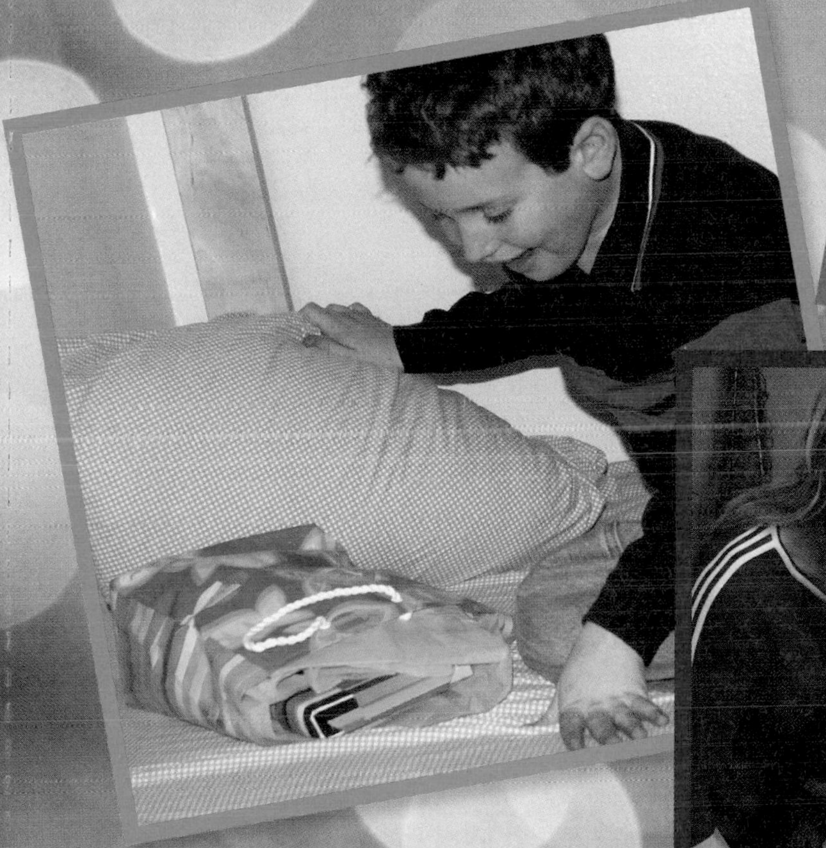

Prayer

Caring Jesus, help me know the Holy Spirit.
I will let him guide me.

A Big Surprise

One day, Jesus' friends were praying. Whoosh! A big wind came from the sky. It filled the house. They saw flames of fire, but they were not afraid. The Holy Spirit had come. Now they could tell the world about Jesus.

adapted from Acts of the Apostles 2:1-4

We call this special day **Pentecost**.

The Holy Spirit Brings Courage

Before this day, Jesus' friends were afraid. They were afraid of people who did not like them. But then the Holy Spirit came. He gave them courage. They were not afraid to talk about Jesus anymore.

Reading God's Word

The Holy Spirit gives us love, joy, and peace.

adapted from Galatians 5:22

The Holy Spirit Is With Us

The Holy Spirit is always with us. He is with us in our **parish**. He is with us when we help others.

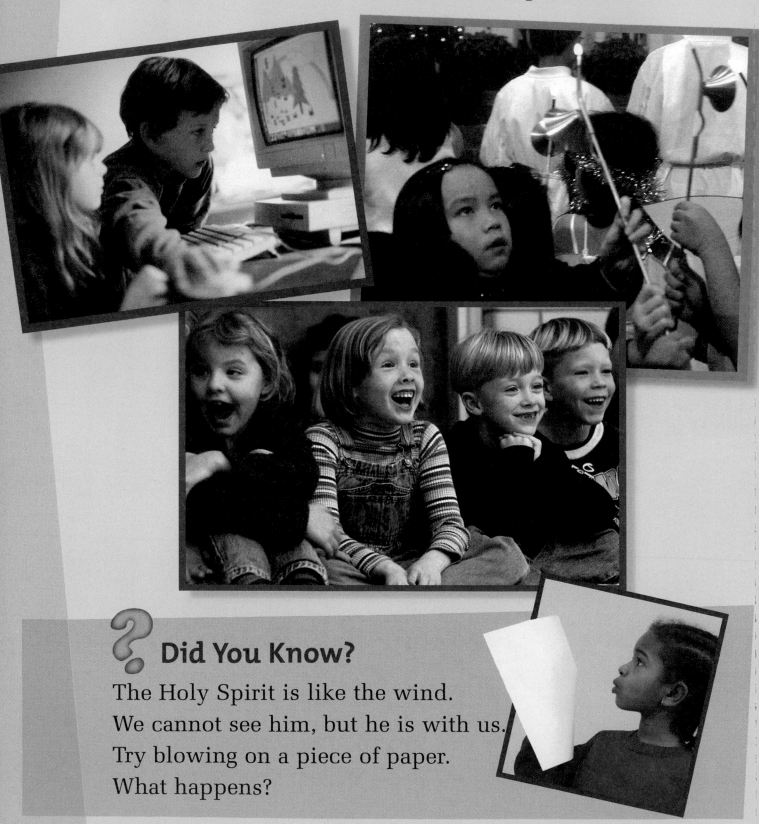

Did You Know?

The Holy Spirit is like the wind.
We cannot see him, but he is with us.
Try blowing on a piece of paper.
What happens?

The Story of Pentecost

Fill in the blank with the correct word.
Look at the pictures for help.

Jesus **praying** **friends** **wind** **fire**

1. Jesus' ___________ were in a room.

2. They were ___________.

3. A big ___________ came from the sky.

4. They saw flames of ___________, but they were not afraid.

5. Then they told the world about ___________.

Prayer

Think of a kind thing you did. The Holy Spirit helped you to be kind. We can pray to the Holy Spirit.

In the name of the Father,
and of the Son,
and of the Holy Spirit.
Amen.

The Holy Spirit lives in your heart. Talk with him. Ask him to be your friend. Ask him to help you be more loving.

Living My Faith

Faith Summary

The Holy Spirit is always with us. He helps us be kind. He helps us be loving.

Words I Learned

parish **Pentecost**

Ways of Being Like Jesus

Think of a kind thing you did. How did the other person feel? How did you feel?

With My Family

Surprise someone! Help your family clean the house. Do a chore, even when it is not your turn.

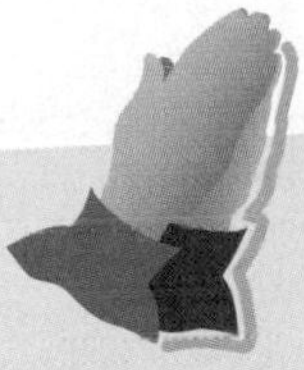

Prayer

Kind Jesus, I am grateful for the gift of the Holy Spirit in my life.

My Response

The Holy Spirit helps us be kind. How will you show the Holy Spirit is with you?

Focus on Faith

The Holy Spirit Guides Us

In the second chapter of the Acts of the Apostles, Luke describes the coming of the Holy Spirit upon the disciples. First the room filled with a sound like a strong wind. Then came tongues of fire that rested on each of them. The disciples left the house alive in the Holy Spirit. The passage gives us no description of this house; the building itself was not significant. The real importance is that from a small gathering of people, numbering only about as many as one could fit into an average home, our Church was born. Clearly, God can accomplish great things from small beginnings. Your child is taking his or her first steps into the life of God's Church. Where will these small beginnings lead?

Dinnertime Conversation Starter

Through Baptism all of us are alive in the Spirit. How well do your family's activities and prayers reflect this fact? Discuss ways in which you might improve.

Our Catholic Heritage

Monsignor John Egan was a priest from the Ravenswood neighborhood in Chicago, Illinois. During the 1960s in Chicago, through the work of the Holy Spirit, he became a prominent force in community organization. He helped promote a general call for a higher social concern by using the Catholic Church and its teachings to combat poverty, while working toward strengthening urban apostolates and inner-city race relations. The committees and organizations he served with included the Chicago Conference on Religion and Race, the Metropolitan Housing and Planning Council Board of Governors, and the Archdiocesan Committee on Poverty. Father Egan's commitment to the Catholic Church and its mission to act as a catalyst in organizing and improving social welfare is an inspiring example of the Holy Spirit in action.

Hints for at Home

Construct a Holy Spirit Wind Catcher with your child. On a piece of sturdy paper or cardboard, trace around a plate. Cut out the circle, and continue cutting it into a spiral. Along the spiral, write the words *The Holy Spirit Moves Us*. Using string, hang your wind catcher in a tree where the wind will move it. Talk with your child about how we cannot see the Holy Spirit any more than we can see the wind, but we still know that the Holy Spirit exists. Explain that through the Holy Spirit we are moved to be kind, loving, and helpful.

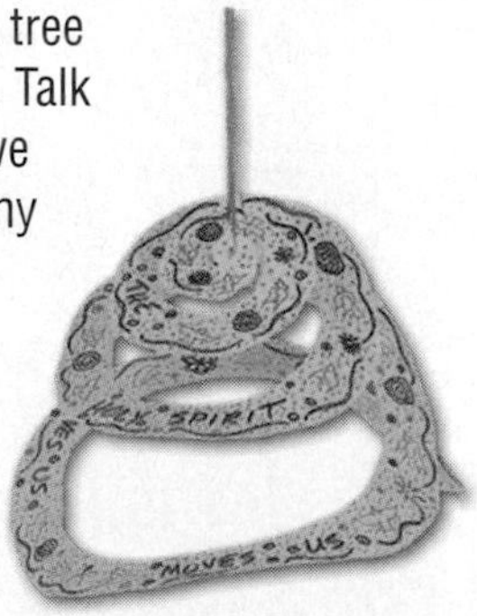

Focus on Prayer

Your child is reviewing the Sign of the Cross. Practice it together, and then discuss a kind act your child performed recently. Praise your child for it, while commenting on how this act revealed the Holy Spirit in your child's heart. Enjoy talking quietly with your child.

Jesus Teaches Us to Share

Session 13

What does it mean to share?
What do you share with others?

What are you showing others when you share with them?

Prayer

Loving Jesus, teach me how to share. I will share your love with others.

Sharing With Others

After Pentecost, Jesus' friends were happy.
They were ready to share Jesus' love.

They ate together and prayed together.
They shared their food and money.
They shared everything they had.
They even shared what they knew about Jesus.
People loved this way of life.
Every day, more people joined them.

adapted from Acts of the Apostles 2:42-47

Friends of Jesus

We call these first friends of Jesus Christ **Christians**. We are Christians too.

Circle the special word inside the word *Christian*.

Christian

How Can I Show I Am Christian?

I can pray **.**

I can share **.**

I can love **others.**

Reading God's Word

Be happy, and share your happiness.

adapted from Philippians 2:18

Sharing and Praying Together

We belong to the **Catholic** Church. As Catholics, we share and pray together. Jesus' friends did this long ago. Jesus' friends still do this today.

We share with our parish.
We share with our families.

What Are We?

Write these letters in the correct blanks. **a c l**

We are

C_tho_i_!

Our Neighbors

Who are our neighbors?

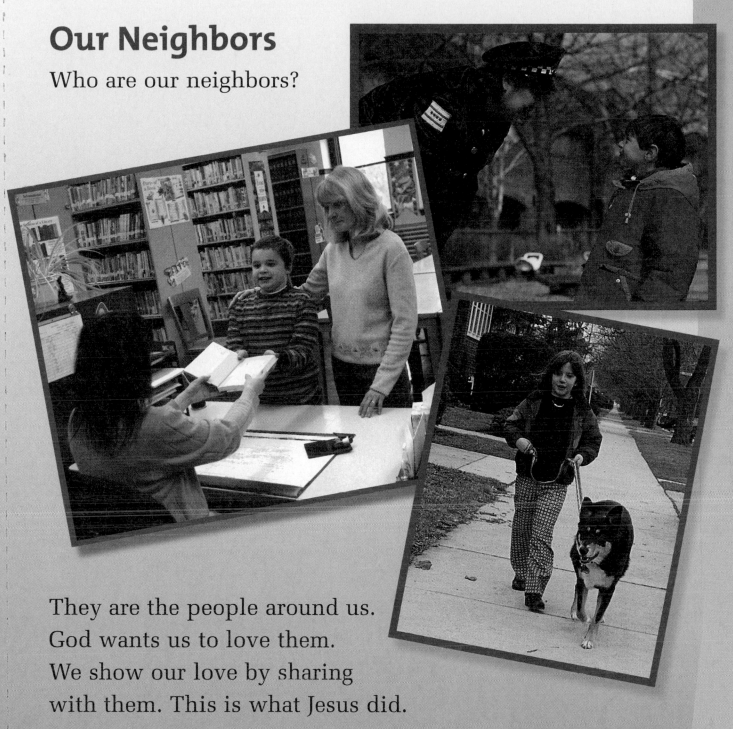

They are the people around us.
God wants us to love them.
We show our love by sharing
with them. This is what Jesus did.

Link to Liturgy

How do we share our love at Mass?
One way is to offer others the sign of peace.

Prayer

This is a special prayer to Jesus.

Thank you, Jesus.
My friend! My brother!
Help me know you more clearly.
Help me love you more dearly.
Help me follow you more nearly.
Amen.

adapted from St. Richard of Chichester's Prayer

Imagine you are with Jesus. Jesus is smiling at you. Tell him how you will love him. Tell him how you will follow him.

Living My Faith

Faith Summary

We belong to the Catholic Church. We show our love by sharing with others.

Words I Learned

Catholic Christian

Ways of Being Like Jesus

Jesus shared what he had. Share a favorite toy or treat with a brother, sister, or friend.

With My Family

We can share by talking. Talk with your family about a time you had fun together.

Prayer

Jesus, my teacher, thank you for teaching me how to share.

My Response

How will you share your love today?

RAISING FAITH-FILLED KIDS

a parent page

Focus on Faith

Discovering Jesus' Community

You are kneeling quietly during Mass on Sunday. People are still receiving Holy Communion. After your personal prayer, you take a little time to reflect on your fellow parishioners. A large family passes by, the children lively and restless. A retired religious sister returns to her place, her walker clicking on the floor. You notice them all: young, elderly, men, women, some with a sparkle in their eyes, some with "Why am I here?" looks on their faces. God calls everyone. Each of us has something extraordinary to offer. What unique gifts do you bring to his community?

Dinnertime Conversation Starter

Your child also brings a unique gift to God's community. Explore with him or her what that gift is. What special gifts do other individuals bring?

In Our Parish

Create a Book-Sharing Box. With your child, decorate a large cardboard box, leaving the top open. Place it in a conspicuous place in your parish. Encourage others to donate books to the sharing box. Use it as a book-swap library: When you take a book, leave a book.

Spirituality in Action

A simple way to demonstrate sharing is by cooking a meal for someone sick or in need. With your child, plan a simple meal, prepare it, and then deliver it together. Thus, you share your food and, more importantly, your company.

Focus on Prayer

Your child is learning a simple version of the Prayer of St. Richard of Chichester. Visit www.FindingGod.org for the wording of this prayer, and pray it together at bedtime.

God Chose Mary

Session 14

A new boy moved in next door. He did not know anyone.

Tina's mom said, "I think he could use a friend. Will you say hello to him?"

Tina thought about it. She knew it would make the boy happy. So she said yes.

When did you do something to make someone else happy?

Prayer

Jesus, help me say yes to God.
I want to love God as Mary did.

An Angel Visits Mary

Mary lived long ago.

One day an angel came to her. The angel's name was Gabriel. God sent Gabriel to Mary.

Mary was afraid.

Gabriel said, "Do not be afraid. You will have a son. You will name him Jesus."

Mary said, "I will do what God wants." Mary said yes to God.

adapted from Luke 1:26-38

Mary Answers God

What did Mary say to God?

Color in the pieces marked with a Y.

God Loved Mary

God chose Mary to be Jesus' mother.
Mary said she wanted to serve God.
Mary said yes to God.

God gave Mary the gift of **grace**.
Grace makes us beautiful to God.

Reading God's Word

Mary said, "God is happy with me. Everyone will call me blessed."

adapted from Luke 1:48

The Mother of God

Mary was the first one to know that Jesus was coming. She loved him very much. She loves us too. We call her the Mother of God.

Did You Know?

Many Catholic churches have a statue of Mary. Can you find one in your church?

Prayer

Mary is important to our Church. We have a special prayer for her.

Hail Mary, full of grace,
the Lord is with you.
Blessed are you among women,
and blessed is the fruit
of your womb, Jesus.
Holy Mary, Mother of God,
pray for us sinners,
now and at the hour of our death.
Amen.

Now quietly think about these words. Tell Mary you are glad she said yes to God.

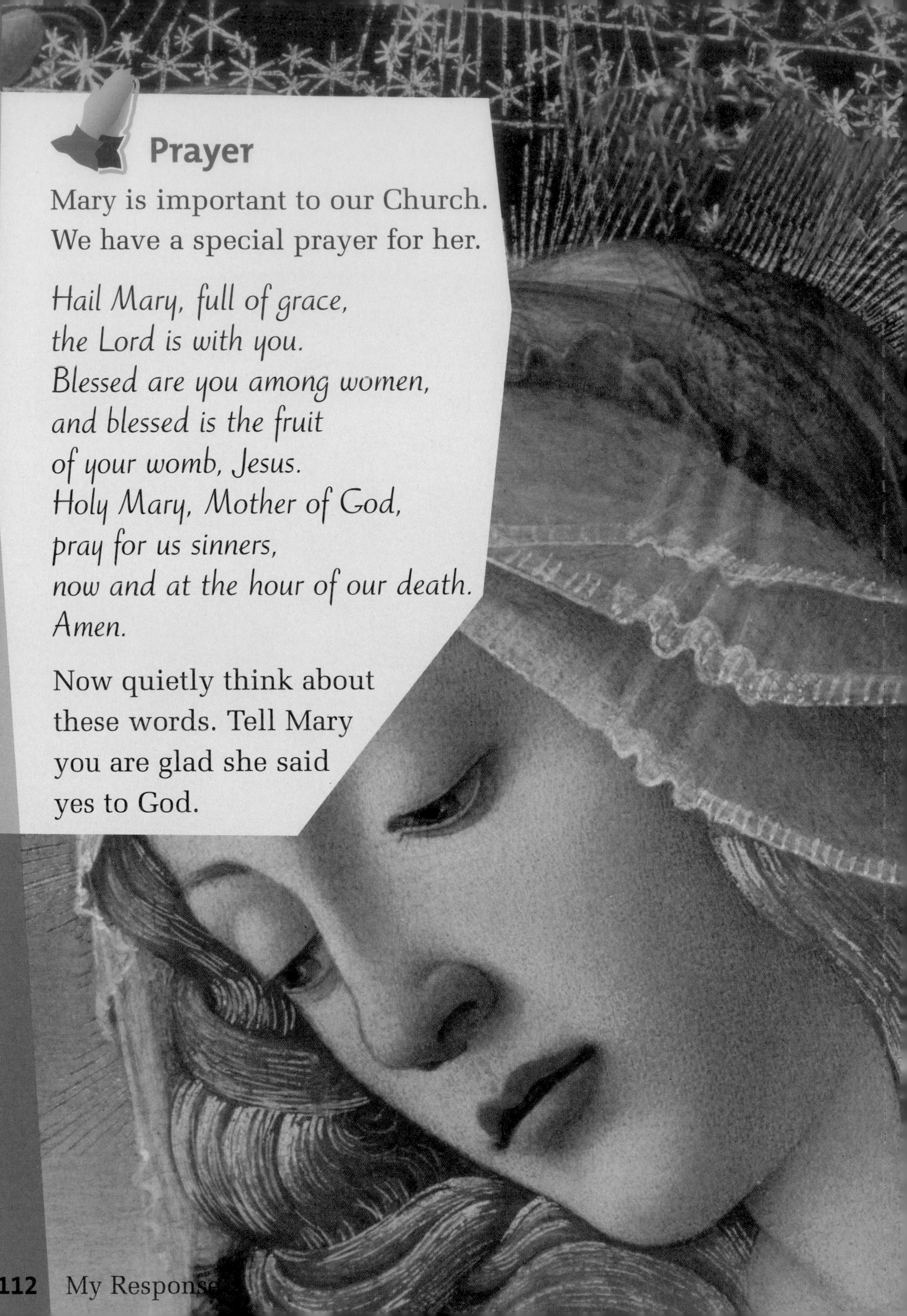

Living My Faith

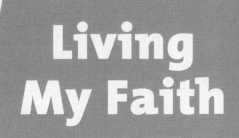

Faith Summary

God chose Mary to be the mother of Jesus. Mary said yes.

Word I Learned

grace

Ways of Being Like Jesus

Jesus was kind to his family. You are like him when you are kind to your family.

With My Family

Who are some special women in your family? Mom? Grandma? An aunt? Do something nice for them to show your love.

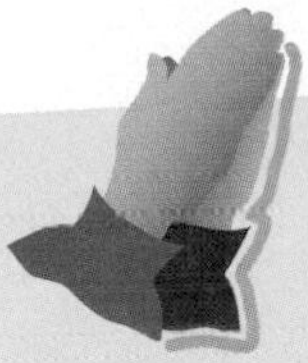

Prayer

Jesus, Son of Mary, thank you for helping me to grow in grace. I will say yes to God each day.

My Response

How can you say yes to God?

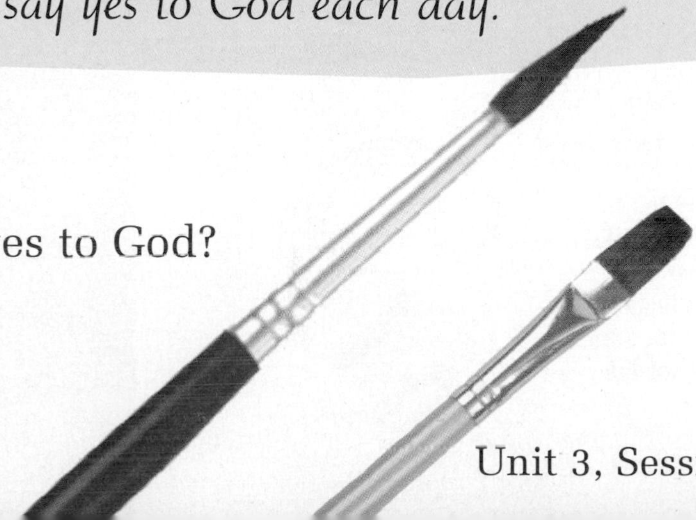

Our Lady Queen of Peace, Hamilton Reed Armstrong

Focus on Faith

Mary in Our Lives

Scholars tell us that Mary was probably in her mid-teens at the time of the Annunciation. This was the normal age for a girl to be betrothed. She was from an otherwise-undistinguished family, living in an occupied country. It is no wonder that Mary questioned God's plan for her; nevertheless, she believed and faced the future confident that God would be with her. We face an unknown future. As we get older and move through life, we discover that things are not as certain as they once seemed. We cannot help but wonder about the world in which we are bringing up our children. Mary faced all these issues with faith and hope. Never be afraid to ask her for help.

Dinnertime Conversation Starter

Although your first grader is quite young, he or she still has decisions to make. Ask your child what decisions he or she had to make today. Explain how present decisions often affect the future.

Hints for at Home

Make a Mary Crown. With your child, collect beautiful flowers and leaves. If fresh flowers are not available, use artificial flowers. Fasten the flowers and leaves to a base, which you can make out of wire or craft stems. When you are finished, place the crown in a special area of your home. Be sure to talk with your child about the importance of Mary in our lives.

In Our Parish

As a family, visit the statue of Mary in your church after Sunday Mass. Encourage your child to talk about the statue. Pause to say a Hail Mary or, perhaps, to light a vigil candle.

Focus on Prayer

Your child is learning the Hail Mary. Pray the prayer together often as a family, and talk about what it means to say yes to God as Mary did. Visit www.FindingGod.org for the words to this prayer.

Review

Session 15

Do you remember Saint Peter?
He loved Jesus very much.

Jesus loved him too. He made
Peter the first leader of the Church.

Prayer

Dear Jesus, please help me follow your call.
I want to lead others to you.

Faith Summary

We find Jesus' friends in the Church. The Church helps us learn to love those around us. The Holy Spirit is with us when we are together.

The Holy Spirit was with Mary. Mary became the Mother of God.

The Fishermen

Characters: Narrator, Jesus, Peter, Andrew, James, John

Narrator:	Peter and Andrew were fishing. Jesus passed by. He called to them.
Jesus:	*Come, follow me. Help me help others.*
Peter:	*But we are fishermen.*
Andrew:	*We have work to do.*
Jesus:	*This will be your new work.*
Peter:	*I will follow you, Jesus.*
Andrew:	*So will I.*

Narrator:	Peter and Andrew walked with Jesus. They came to James and John. Jesus called to them.
Jesus:	*Come, follow me. Help me help others.*
James:	*But we are fishermen.*
John:	*We have work to do.*
Jesus:	*This will be your new work.*
James:	*I will follow you, Jesus.*
John:	*So will I.*
Narrator:	All four men followed Jesus. They followed him together. They spent their lives helping others know Jesus.

Prayer Service

Leader: *Let us bless ourselves.*

All: *In the name of the Father,*
and of the Son,
and of the Holy Spirit.
Amen.

Leader: *Jesus asks you to help others.*
How will you answer him?
Will you say yes to Jesus?

Talk to Jesus in your heart.

Let us ask Mary to watch over us as we follow her Son.

All: *Hail Mary, full of grace,*
the Lord is with you.
Blessed are you among women,
and blessed is the fruit
of your womb, Jesus.
Holy Mary, Mother of God,
pray for us sinners,
now and at the hour of our death.
Amen.

Living My Faith

Ways of Being Like Jesus

People may look different. But we are all the same inside. Be kind to everyone you meet.

With My Family

Your community starts with your family. How many people can you name in your family? Remember your aunts, uncles, and cousins.

Prayer

Dear Jesus, I am happy to be one of your followers.

My Response

How will you make someone feel special?

Meeting Jesus

Unit 4

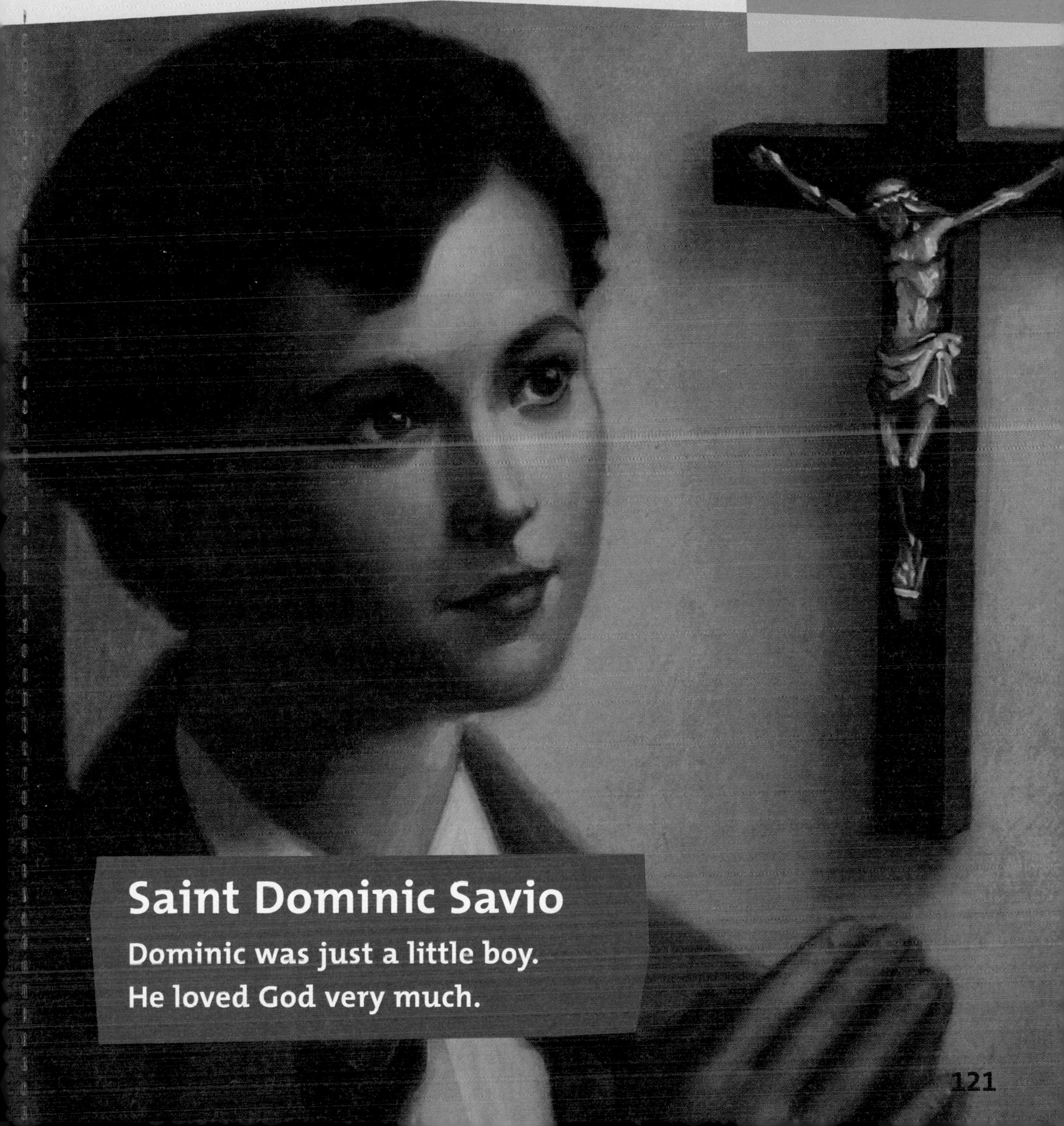

Saint Dominic Savio

Dominic was just a little boy. He loved God very much.

Saint Dominic

Once Dominic's mom could not find him. She looked everywhere.

She could not believe it. He was busy praying!

Another time Dominic saw some boys fighting. Dominic said, "Stop! You are not like Jesus if you fight." The boys thought about what Dominic said. Then they walked away as friends.

Dominic Savio was just a little boy. He showed his love for God in a big way.

Jesus in Our Lives

Session 16

Lola cares for Dad.

Nick gives Mom a kiss.

Hannah adopts a kitten.

What other signs do we use to show our love?

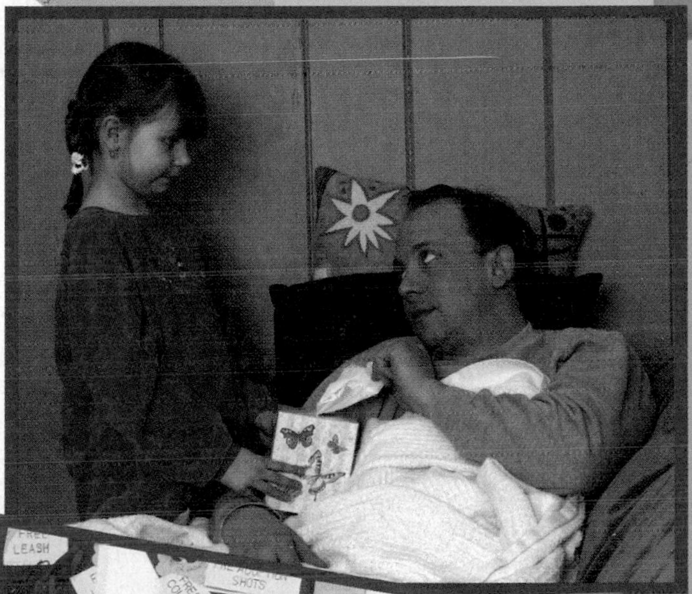

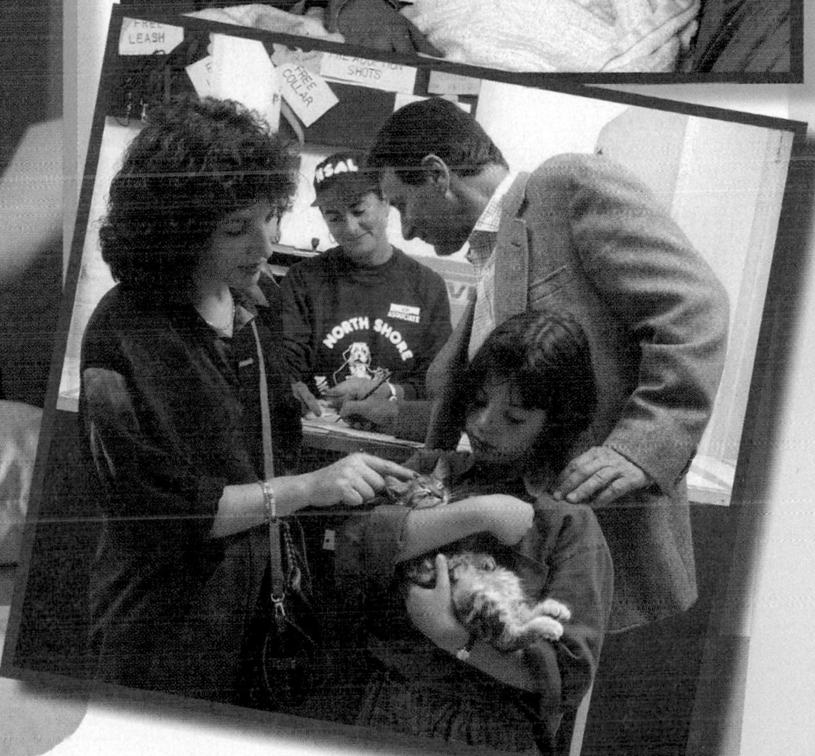

Prayer

Jesus, my friend, help me see the signs of your love. Then I will know you are near.

Jesus Loves Children

People brought children to see Jesus. But Jesus' friends said, "Do not bother him with children."

Jesus heard this. He was upset. He said, "Bring the children to me. They are very special people."

Jesus hugged the children. He placed his hands on them. Then he blessed them.

adapted from Mark 10:13-16

Children Are Special

Children were special to Jesus. He wanted everyone to know this. So he showed them. He gave them signs of his love.

Signs of Jesus' Love

Look at the picture of Jesus and the children. What is Jesus doing? How is he showing his love? Write your answers in the hearts.

Jesus Loves Us

Jesus gave the children signs of his love. Today we have signs that he loves us too. We call them **sacraments.**

Sacraments give us God's grace. Sacraments help us live the way God wants us to live. They bring us closer to Jesus.

Did You Know?

Jesus gave us the sacraments.

Caring for Our Spirit

Priests share signs of Jesus' love. They help us celebrate the sacraments. They guide our Church.

Reading God's Word

Enjoy God's goodness. Let him protect you. Then you will be happy.

adapted from Psalm 34:9

Prayer

Imagine that you are sitting next to Jesus. He puts his hand on your forehead. He blesses you. He smiles at you. He takes time with you.

Jesus wants you to know that you are special. How does knowing that make you feel? What will you say to Jesus? Will you tell him you love him? Will you thank him? Be still with Jesus. Enjoy being with him.

Living My Faith

Faith Summary

Jesus gives us signs of his love. We call them sacraments. They help us to live the way God wants us to live.

Words I Learned

priest **sacrament**

Ways of Being Like Jesus

Show signs of your love.
Give someone a big smile.
Let someone else go first when you play.

With My Family

Show a brother, sister, or cousin that you care. Play nicely with him or her.

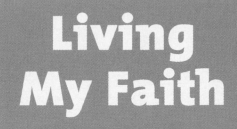

Prayer

Dear Jesus, thank you for showing me signs that you are near.

My Response

What signs of love will you show this week?

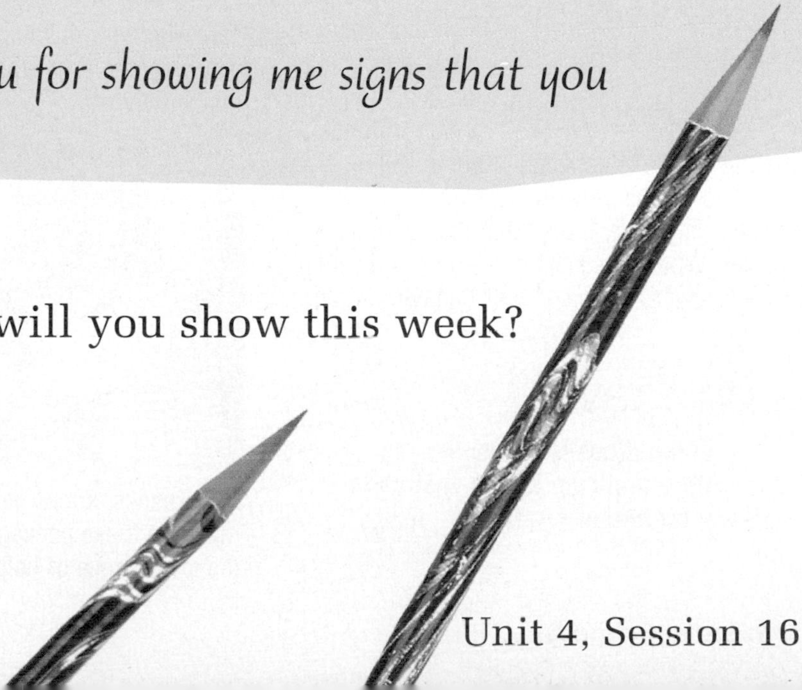

RAISING FAITH-FILLED KIDS

a parent page

Focus on Faith

Bringing Our Children to Jesus

One of the most touching scenes in the New Testament is in the Gospel of Mark, in which Jesus shows his love for and devotion to children. During this event, people were bringing their children to Jesus for his blessing, but his disciples tried to send them away. Jesus was upset by the actions of his disciples and insisted that they bring the children to him. Jesus then embraced and blessed the children. As parents, we have a daily opportunity to help our children discover who Jesus is for them. In what ways do we act as the disciples did, keeping our children away from Jesus? In what ways are we bringing Jesus and our children together?

Dinnertime Conversation Starter

Encourage your child to bring friends into your home and discuss with him or her ways to make friends feel welcome and special.

Hints for at Home

Being Like Jesus
I was kind.
I helped.
I played nicely.
I listened.
I was polite.

Discuss with your child the many ways we show others signs of our love and caring. Then, together, make a chart for your child to track the times that he or she is especially thoughtful or kind. Whenever he or she performs a kind or considerate deed, fill in the appropriate box with a mark or a sticker. When the chart is filled up, present your child with a reward for his or her behavior.

Spirituality in Action

Talk with your child about people who are homeless and ways we can show them signs of caring. Help can be given in a variety of ways, whether it be through a donation of time, supplies, or money. A simple way to get involved is by making care packages of common items and delivering them to shelters. Toothbrushes, toothpaste, soap, hairbrushes, socks, and towels are always useful. As you make up these packages together, discuss with your child the importance of helping others.

Focus on Prayer

Praying the Sign of the Cross is a good way to show Christian faith. Practicing it with your child will make it easier for him or her to learn it.

Joining God's Family

Session
17

How do you use water? How does it taste when you are thirsty? How does it feel on a hot day?

Water is special. It brings life to plants and animals. It brings life to us too.

Prayer

Jesus, my brother, teach me that I am part of God's family.

Followers of Jesus

One day Peter was talking about Jesus.

Many people heard Peter's words. They asked, "How can we follow Jesus?"

"Love God. Join his family," said Peter.

And many did as Peter said. They followed Jesus. They joined God's family.

adapted from Acts of the Apostles 2:37-41

Our First Sacrament

We became followers of Jesus.
We received **Baptism.** It is a sacrament.

What happens when we are baptized?
We become adopted children of God.
We become part of God's family.
We receive the Holy Spirit.

Once we were small. A priest poured blessed water on us. Now we are older. Now we can bless ourselves. We use **holy water.** It reminds us of our Baptism.

Special People

Special people come to our Baptism.
We call them **godparents.**
They help our parents.

How do godparents help?

They help teach us about God.
They help us lead good lives.

Reading God's Word

Teach everyone about me. Baptize them in the name of the Father, and of the Son, and of the Holy Spirit.

adapted from Matthew 28:19

What Is the Word?

Which sentence matches the picture?
Write the number in the box.

1. These people help teach us about God.

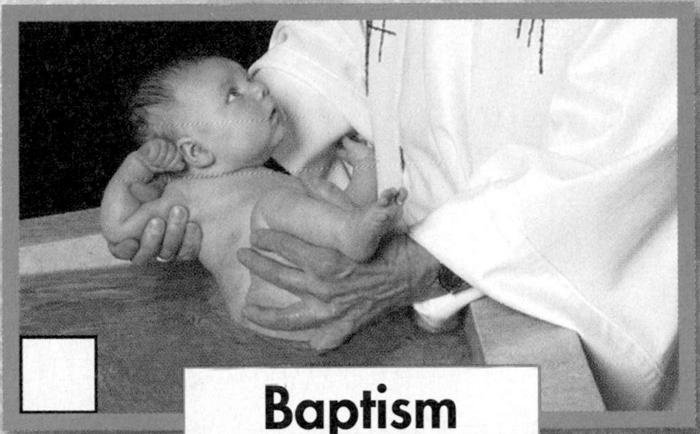

Baptism

2. We become followers of Jesus with this sacrament.

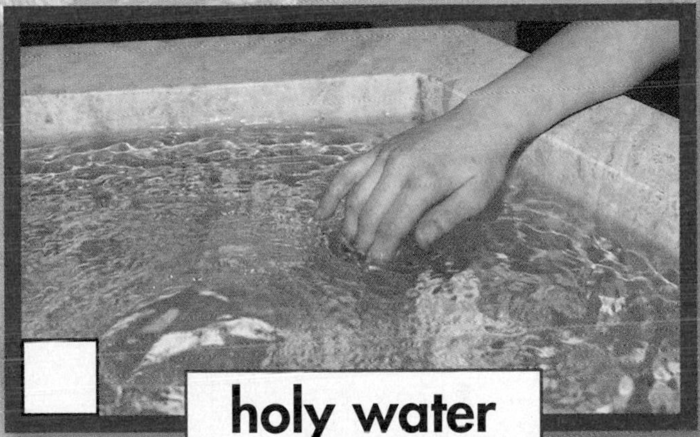

holy water

3. We use this to remind us of our Baptism.

godparents

Did You Know?

Every Catholic church has holy water. Where is the holy water in your church?

Prayer

Keep in mind that God our Father created you. Jesus his Son loves you. The Holy Spirit gives you the gift of peace.

You were welcomed into God's family when you were baptized. You can show that you are part of his family. You can pray the Sign of the Cross.

In the name of the Father,
and of the Son,
and of the Holy Spirit.
Amen.

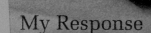

Living My Faith

Faith Summary

In Baptism we become part of God's family. We receive the Holy Spirit.

Words I Learned

Baptism **godparent** **holy water**

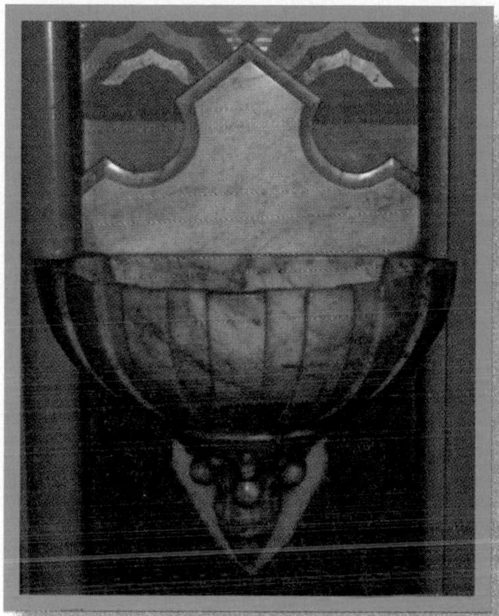

Ways of Being Like Jesus

Be a special friend to someone.

With My Family

Dip your hand in the holy water.
Pray the Sign of the Cross.
Remember that you are baptized.

Prayer

Jesus, my friend, thank you for the gift of Baptism. Your love makes me special.

My Response

How will you show you are happy to be part of God's family?

RAISING FAITH-FILLED KIDS

a parent page

Focus on Faith

An Example of Faith

A businessman looked out his window every morning at 7:30. He saw the same woman walking up the hill to the Catholic Church for Mass. He had no time for God in his life. Everyone in his circle was agnostic. But every day, rain or shine, this woman passed by his window. What was it that gave her such faith and devotion? He waited for the day when she would miss Mass. Then, one morning an especially vicious ice storm hit the area. Would this be the day? The woman could not possibly walk up the hill. The businessman was stunned, though, when he saw her crawling up the hill, trying not to slip on the ice. He was so moved at the sight of the woman's determination and devotion that he told his astonished family that he was going to become Catholic. One woman's faith showed him what was missing in his life.

Dinnertime Conversation Starter

Speak with your child about faithfulness—from beginning each day with prayer to attending Mass to caring for the needs of others—and the power of setting a good example.

Our Catholic Heritage

Holy wells, which are especially prevalent throughout Great Britain and Ireland, have been used for hundreds of years as places of worship and veneration. Some wells predate the birth of Christ and were used originally as places of pagan worship. As Christianity spread throughout the region, the wells were converted quickly to sites associated with Christianity. Many people believe the water from these wells has healing properties. For hundreds of years, they have made pilgrimages to the wells to drink or bathe in the sacred water. Offerings such as coins and clothing can be found at many of these wells. Some of the more famous wells are St. Winifred's in Wales and St. Feidhlimh's in Ireland.

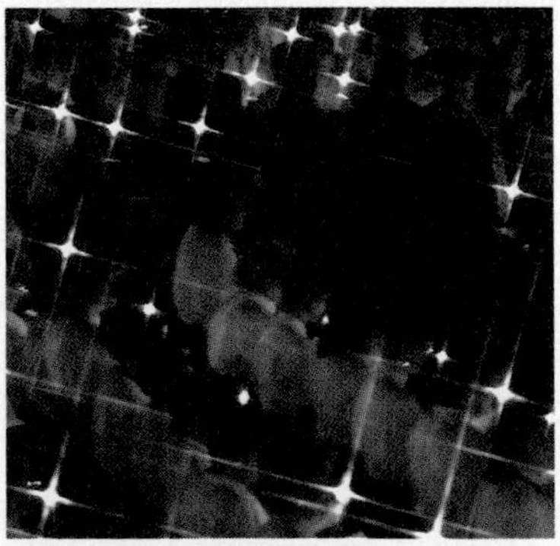

In Our Parish

Take your child to a Baptism during the Easter Vigil or on another occasion. Point out symbols to look for, such as water (new life), oil (strength), white garment (purity), and the Baptismal candle (light of Christ). While in the church, take this opportunity to fill a small jar with holy water, which you can keep in your home. Talk with your child about how holy water is a reminder of Baptism.

Focus on Prayer

Your child is learning the significance of using holy water while praying the Sign of the Cross: together they are a reminder of our Baptism. Prompt your child to use holy water to bless himself or herself when entering or exiting the church.

Celebrating Jesus

Session 18

Neal and his family eat together. They share. They pray.

When did you have a special meal? Who was there? Why was it special?

Prayer

Jesus, help me know you are always with me.

A Special Meal With Jesus

Jesus was with his friends. They were having a meal.

Jesus took bread. He blessed it. He broke it. Then he shared it with his friends. He said, "Eat this. Remember me."

Then Jesus took a cup of wine. He blessed it. He shared it with his friends. He said, "Drink this. I will always be with you."

adapted from Luke 22:19-20

The Last Supper

The meal Jesus shared is called the **Last Supper.** It was a special meal.

We have a special meal at Mass. Jesus is with us in a special way.

Link to Liturgy

The priest consecrates the bread and wine. The bread and wine becomes Jesus' Body and Blood.

Our Special Meal

Every Sunday we go to Mass.
What do we do at Mass?

We remember Jesus.
We have a special meal.
We show our love for
one another.

Then the priest says
important words.
He tells us to love
and serve God.

Reading God's Word

Whatever you do, do it to praise God.

adapted from 1 Corinthians 10:31

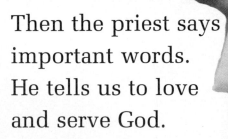

My Special Meal

What would it be like if you had a special meal?
Who would be there? What would you eat?
Finish the picture. Then color it.

Prayer

Prayer Before Meals

We pray a special prayer before we eat. We fold our hands. We think about all God gives us.

Bless us, O Lord,
and these your gifts
which we are about to receive
from your goodness.
Through Christ our Lord.
Amen.

Prayer After Meals

We pray a special prayer after we eat. We fold our hands. We think about how blessed we are.

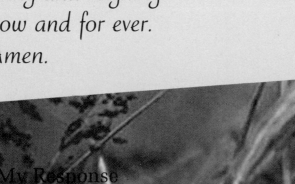

We give you thanks
for all your gifts,
almighty God,
living and reigning
now and for ever.
Amen.

Living My Faith

Faith Summary

We go to Mass every Sunday. We share a special meal. Jesus is with us in his Body and Blood.

Word I Learned

Last Supper

Ways of Being Like Jesus

Tell your friends and family how special they are to you.

With My Family

Help plan a special meal with your family.

Prayer

Jesus, my friend, thank you for giving yourself to me.

My Response

How can you make every meal special?

RAISING FAITH-FILLED KIDS

a parent page

Focus on Faith

Making Memories

A mother asked her grown daughters what some of the happiest memories from their childhood were. Both of them enthusiastically replied that it was the times when the family went camping; they treasured watching their mother create a little piece of home around the tent and the picnic table at the campsite. They enjoyed having no phones or television sets and leaving the daily concerns of life behind for a few days. Memories such as these are the glue that bind a family and make it strong. These memories depend on feelings of togetherness, not on money or material goods. What memories are you creating for your children today?

Dinnertime Conversation Starter

Ask your child about his or her favorite memory of something your family did. What makes it so special and memorable? Share your favorite family memory as well.

Our Catholic Heritage

Tell your child stories about Catholics who truly show they love and serve the Lord. Use examples of Catholics from your own parish or area or research Web sites such as the one for the Maryknoll Missionaries. **(www.maryknoll.org)**

Hints for at Home

Make Origami Folded Napkins. Talk with your child about how we grow closer to one another when we share meals together. On the finished, folded napkin, write the name of a guest and the words *I will always be with you.*

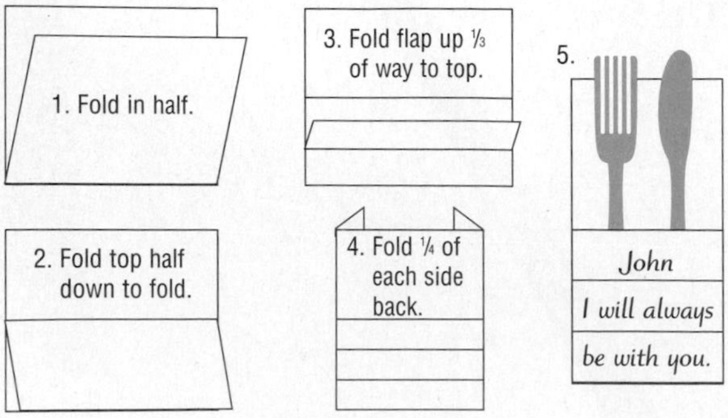
1. Fold in half.
2. Fold top half down to fold.
3. Fold flap up ⅓ of way to top.
4. Fold ¼ of each side back.
5.
John
I will always
be with you.

Focus on Prayer

Pray with your child at mealtimes. Talk with your child about why we pray before and after we share a meal.

Listening to Our Father

Session 19

When have you had a special quiet time? What did you think about? How did you feel?

Prayer

Dear Jesus, help me to be still and to listen when I pray.

Elijah Listens for God

Elijah loved God. He wanted to be alone with him. So he went to a cave. God said, "Go outside. Listen for me. I will be passing by."

Whoosh! A great wind blew. But Elijah could not hear God. Roar! A loud earthquake shook the ground. Elijah could not hear God. Hiss! A fire lit up the sky. Elijah still could not hear God.

Elijah stood very still. Then he heard something. It was a tiny whisper. He listened closely. It was God talking to him.

adapted from 1 Kings 19:9-13

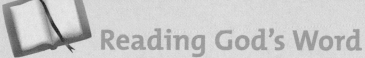

Reading God's Word

Listen to my Father. Learn from him. Then you will come to me.

adapted from John 6:45

Where Can We Find God?

God is always with us. He is everywhere. He wants us to talk to him. He wants us to listen to him. But we need to be quiet to hear him. This is what Elijah did.

Quiet Places

Think about quiet places. Which is your favorite? Draw a picture of it.

Praying to God

What do we tell God?
We tell him we are happy.
We tell him we are sad.
We can tell God anything!

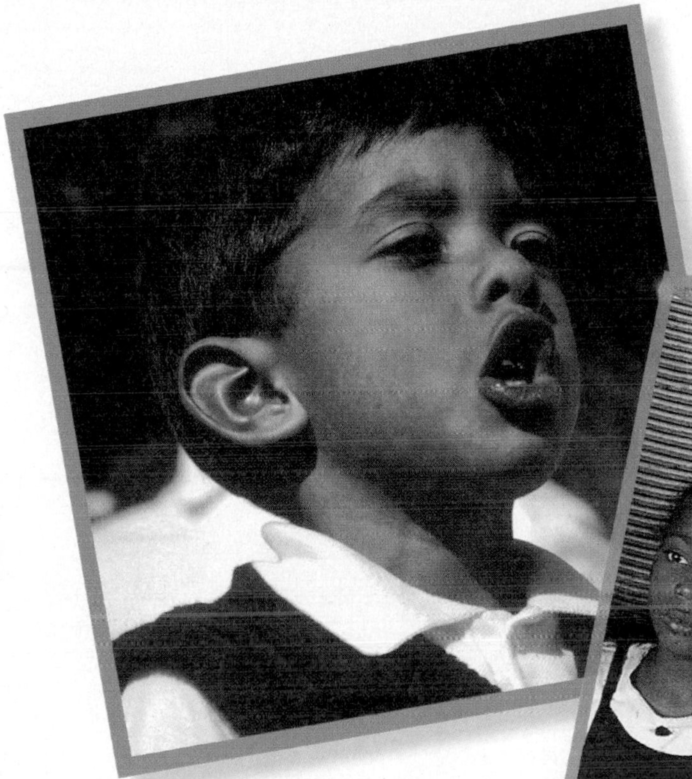

How do we pray?
We use words.
We sing songs.
We use gestures.
We listen to God.

Did You Know?

We can pray anytime and anywhere.

Prayer

Elijah wanted to hear God.
Loud sounds filled the air.
Then he listened closely.
He heard a small sound.
It was God talking to him.

Think about the sounds you hear every day. What are some small sounds around you? Falling rain? Rustling leaves? Soft whispers?

Now be very quiet, as Elijah was. Listen for God. He is all around you. Tell him you will always listen for what he wants you to know.

Living My Faith

Faith Summary

God is everywhere. We may need to listen closely to hear him. We can always pray to him.

Ways of Being Like Jesus

Jesus always made time to pray. Find a quiet time each day, and pray to God.

With My Family

With your family, make a special quiet place. It could be near a window, in your bedroom, or in your yard.

Prayer

Dear God, thank you for teaching me to listen for you. Now I know you are everywhere.

My Response

Where will your quiet place be?

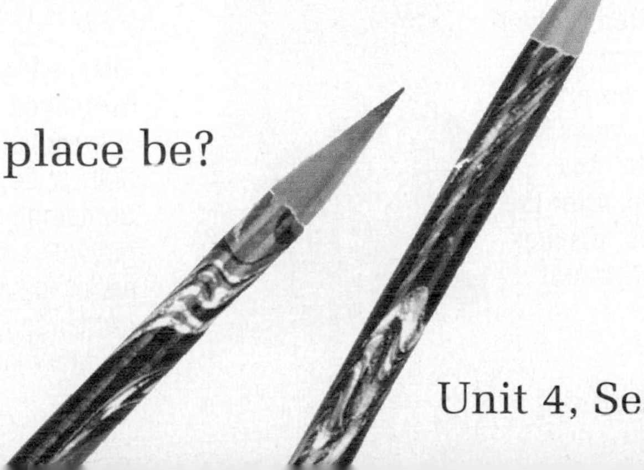

Focus on Faith

Listening to God

The prophet Elijah, hiding in a cave from his enemies, wondered where God was in his life. God spoke to him and told him to go outside the cave because God would be passing by. Just then, a great, strong wind came, followed by an earthquake and then a fire. Elijah, however, could not find God in any of these. Soon came a tiny whispering sound, and it was through this quiet sound that Elijah really heard God. This story teaches us a profound truth: God is always speaking to us, but we have to quiet down to hear him. Through silence our prayers move beyond words to heart-to-heart conversations with God. As we help our children learn to pray, we can also be examples of listening love.

Dinnertime Conversation Starter

Amid all of the family's obligations and activities, when can your family find quiet time? Talk with your family about a good time and place in your lives for "God time."

Hints for at Home

Create a Quiet Corner. With your child choose a quiet, tranquil area of your home that can be used as his or her own private meditative space. It can be as simple as a corner of your child's bedroom or as elaborate as a tree house. Assist your child in making this a comfortable, spiritual, and enjoyable place by adding pillows, books, a reading lamp, pictures, and a Bible. Talk with him or her about the importance of having a special place in which to talk to God and appreciate quiet time. This is also a perfect place for your child to read, write, color, and do other solitary activities.

Focus on Prayer

Your child is learning about all the different forms prayer can take. Physically, we pray to God through reading, singing, kneeling, and genuflecting. Verbally, we pray to God by praising him, thanking him, asking him for help, and telling him we are sorry. After the next Mass you celebrate, discuss with your child all the different ways you prayed.

Spirituality in Action

Men and women who pursue a life of silence, meditation, and prayer are called contemplatives. The contemplative way of life encourages prayer to its highest degree, while strengthening the bond with God. Contemplative orders vary in the degree to which they practice silence. Although silence is a sacrifice, followers of this way of life realize they receive a great deal in exchange. Their perspectives on life, humanity, and God take on richer and deeper meanings.

Review

Session
20

Signs of Jesus are all around us. All we need to do is look closely.

Prayer

Loving Jesus, help me look for signs of your love.
I want to know you are near.

Faith Summary

Jesus gave us signs. They are signs of his love. They tell us he is with us. We call them sacraments.

The first sacrament we receive is Baptism. It makes us a part of God's family.

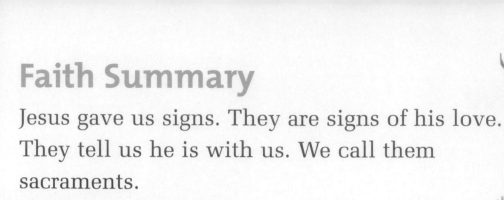

Jesus is with us at Mass. He is with us in his Body and Blood.

God is everywhere. He is always with us. We need to listen closely to hear him.

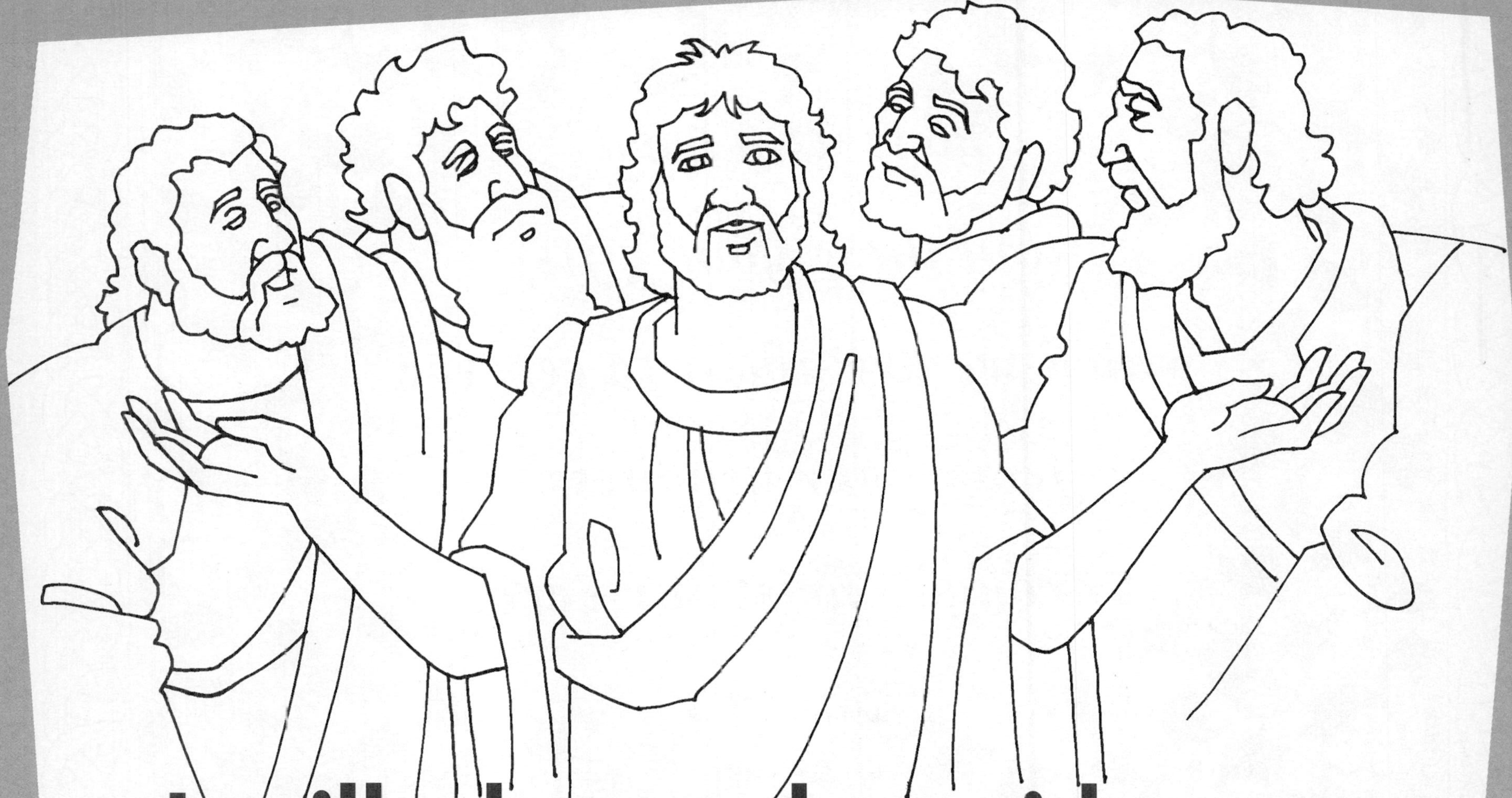

I will always be with you.

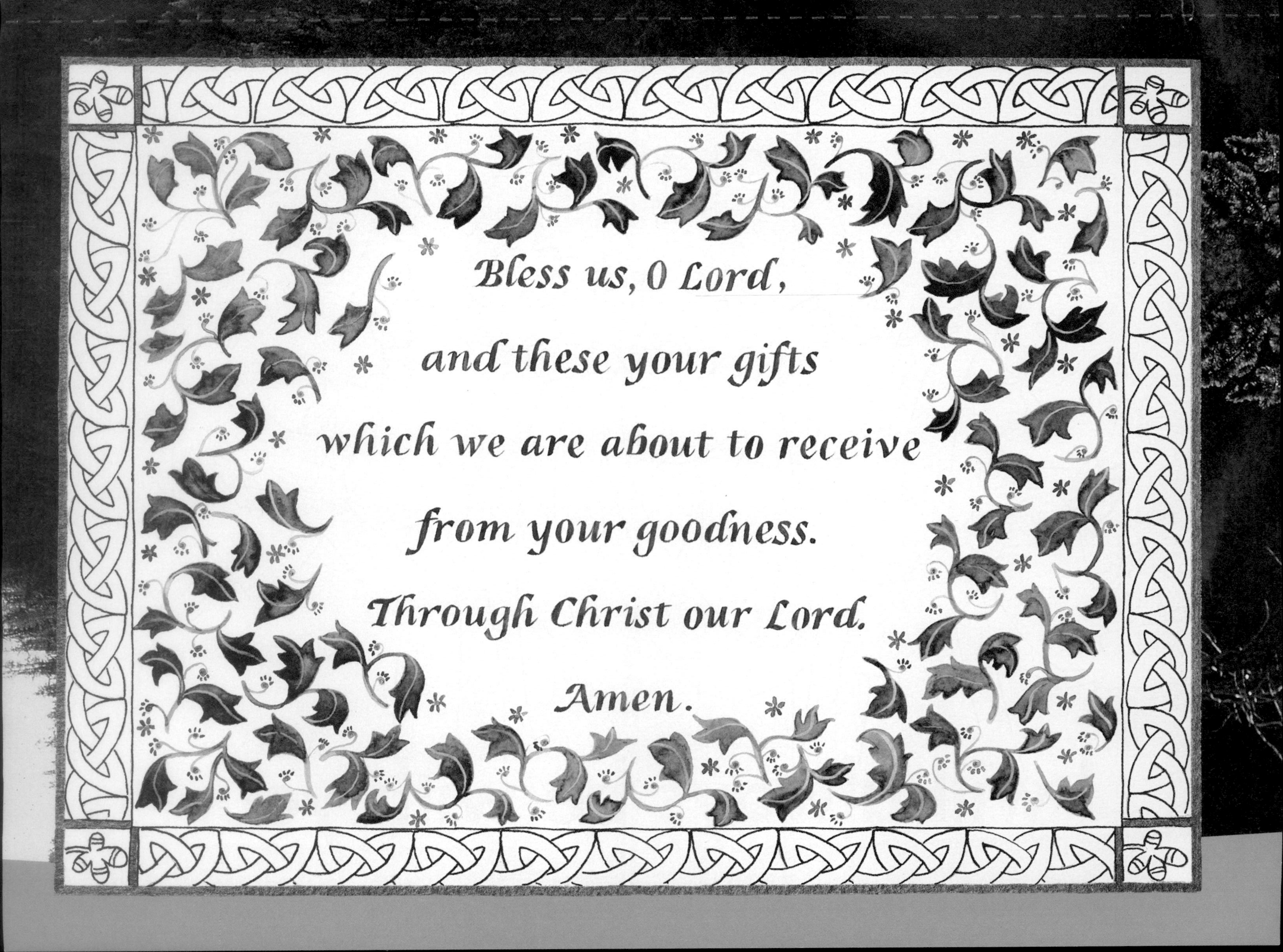
Bless us, O Lord,
and these your gifts
which we are about to receive
from your goodness.
Through Christ our Lord.
Amen.

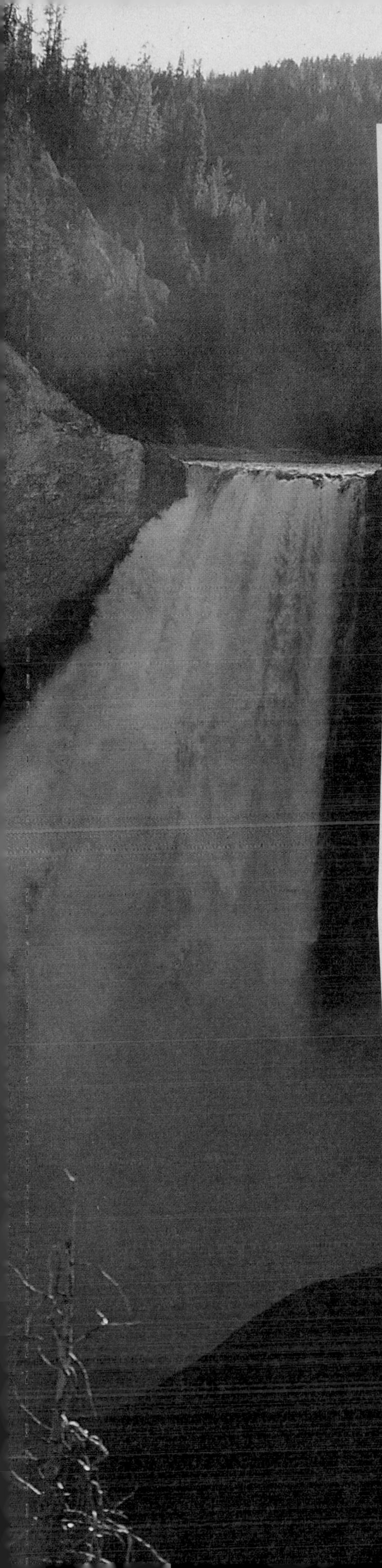

Prayer Service

Leader: *Let us pray the Sign of the Cross.*

Holy water reminds us of our Baptism.

A reading from the Gospel of Matthew.

Jesus said, "Make all the people followers of God. Baptize them in the name of the Father, and of the Son, and of the Holy Spirit."

[adapted from Matthew 28:19]

The gospel of the Lord.

All: *Praise to you, Lord Jesus Christ.*

Leader: *God welcomes us into his family. Let us thank him.*

All: *Glory be to the Father,*
and to the Son,
and to the Holy Spirit.
As it was in the beginning,
is now, and ever shall be,
world without end.
Amen.

Living My Faith

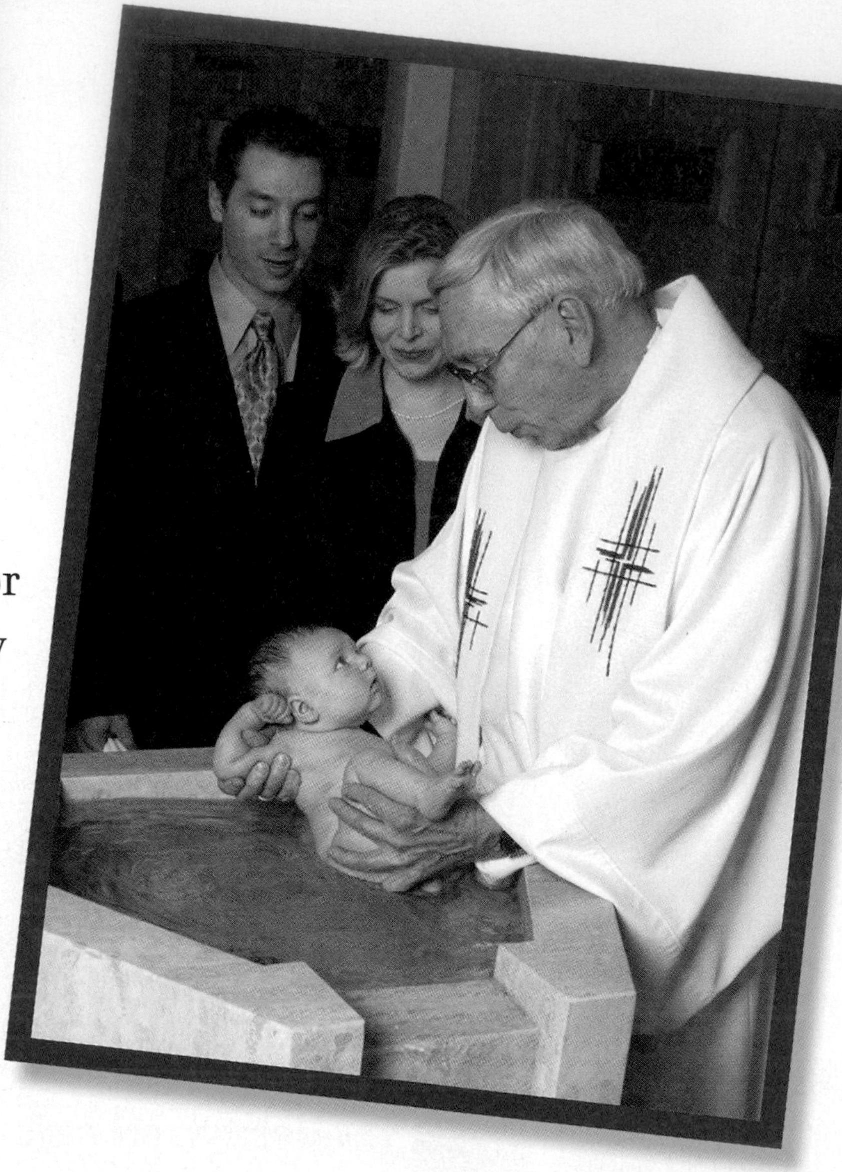

Ways of Being Like Jesus

Jesus told us that he would always care for us. Show your family you care for them.

With My Family

Ask your parents about your baptism. What do they remember?

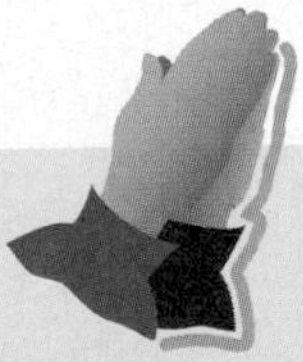

Prayer

Dear Jesus, thank you for giving us the sacraments as signs of your love.

My Response

When will you make special time to listen to God?

Living Like Jesus

Unit 5

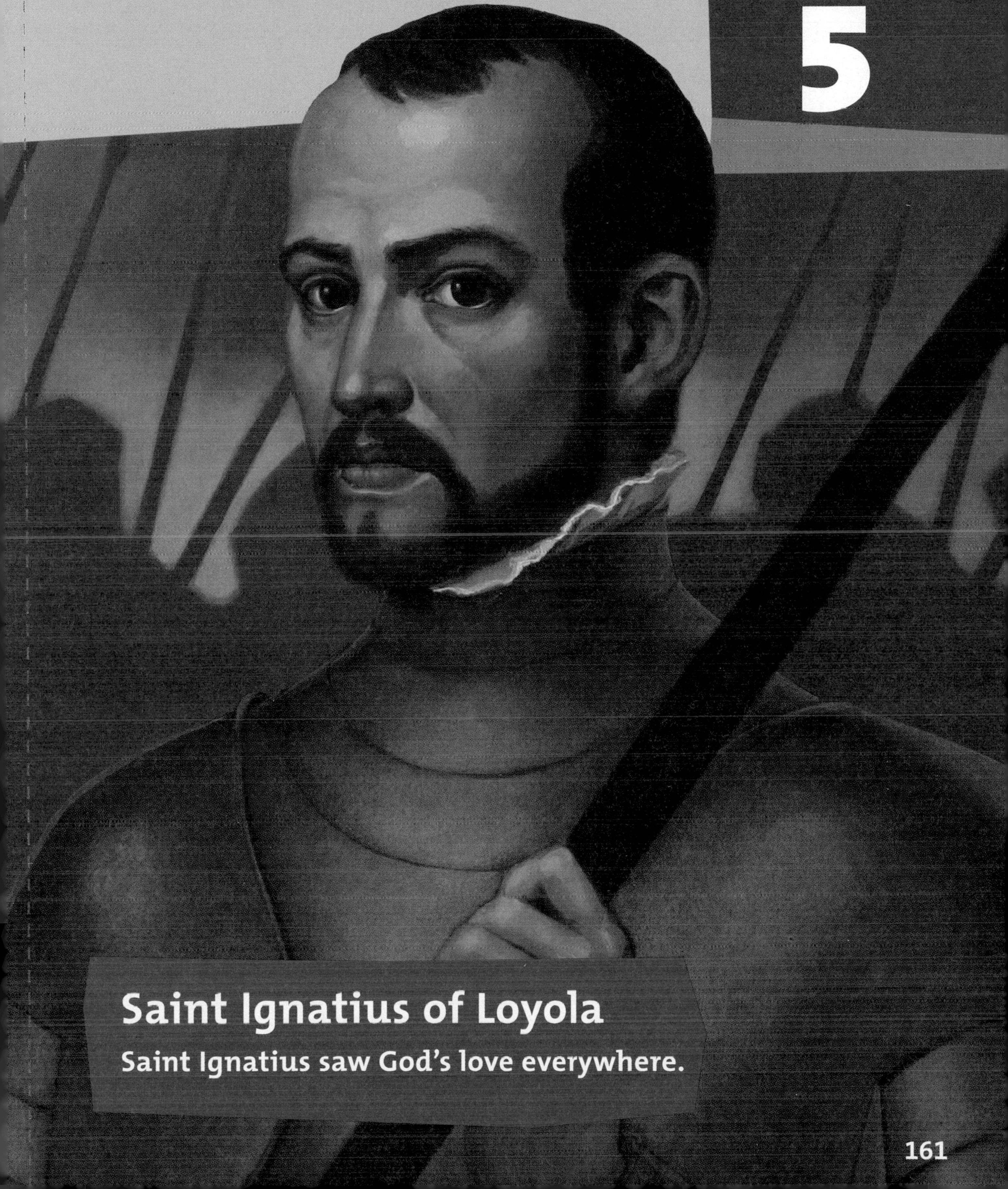

Saint Ignatius of Loyola

Saint Ignatius saw God's love everywhere.

Saint Ignatius

Ignatius was born long ago. He was a brave soldier. He did not think of God often.

One day he got hurt. As he was healing, he read. He prayed. He learned about God. Slowly he began to change.

Ignatius made a decision. He chose to live like Jesus. So he obeyed God's wishes. He cared for others. He loved his family. He loved God's world. Now God came first in his life.

Ignatius became one of God's greatest followers.

Making Good Decisions

Session 21

What is a rule?
Why do we have rules?
Rules keep us safe.
Rules keep us happy.
Rules help us live in peace.

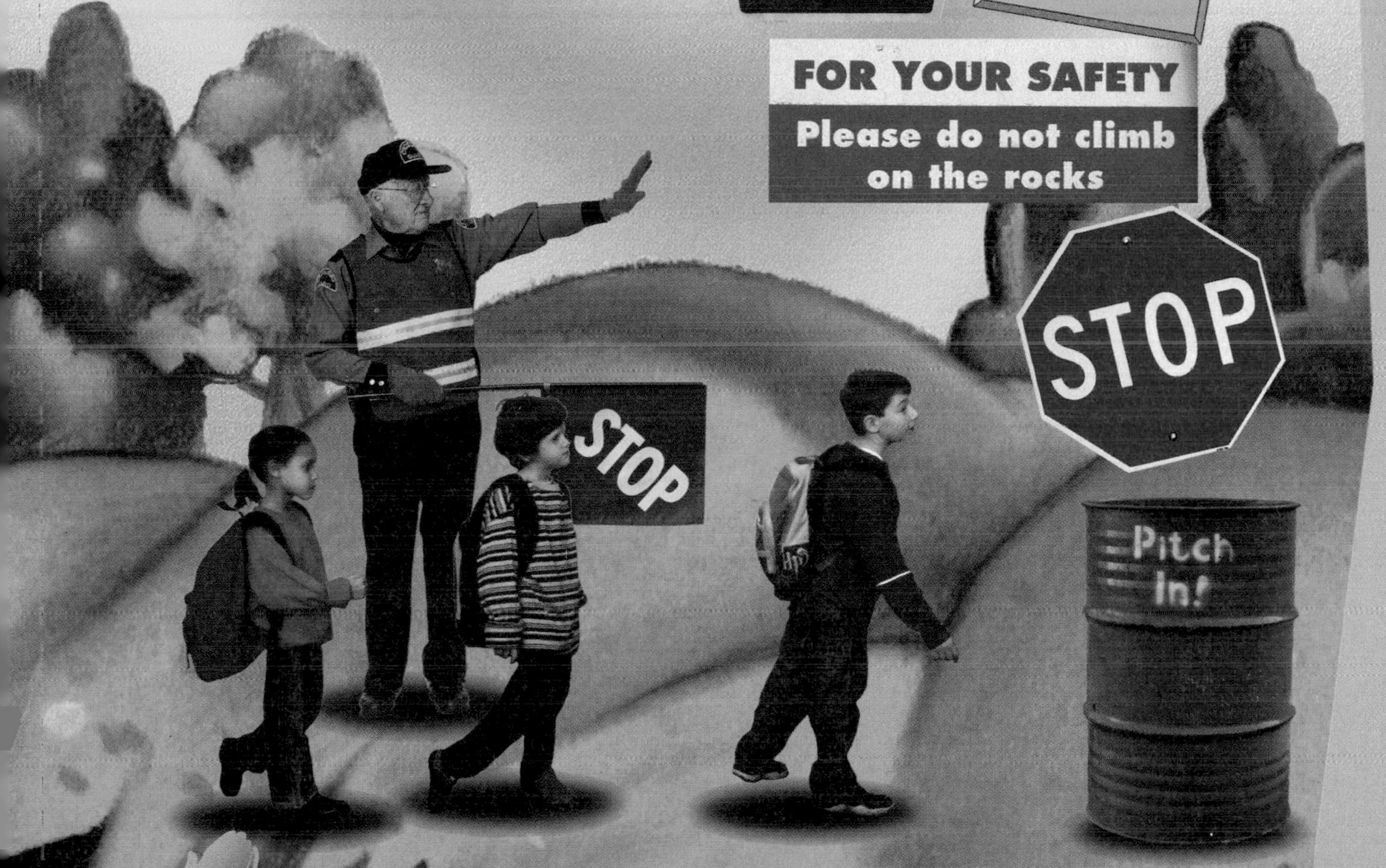

Prayer

Jesus, my guide, teach me to do what is right.
Then I will be happy.

God's Rules

God gives us rules too. We call them **commandments.**

God said, "This is how you can show me your love. Make me important in your life. Use my name in nice ways. Make Sunday a special day."

Then God said, "This is how you can show others your love. Obey your parents. Be kind to others. Take only what belongs to you. Tell the truth. Be happy with what you have."

adapted from Exodus 20:1-17

Decisions

What are some decisions you have made?

Did you **decide** to take time to talk to God?
Did you **decide** to be kind to someone?
Did you **decide** to follow school rules?

We make decisions every day. It is not always easy to choose the right thing. God will always help us. That is why he gave us commandments.

Did You Know?

God will always help us follow his commandments.

How to Make Good Decisions

How can we make good decisions?
We can ask three questions.

Good Decisions

I can make good decisions!

What Should You Do?

Read each group of sentences. For a good decision draw a ☺. For a bad decision draw a ☹.

Mom asks you to pick up your toys. You do it right away.

You find some money. It is not yours. You take it anyway.

You did not do your homework. Your teacher asks you about it. You tell the truth.

Reading God's Word

People asked Jesus, "What is the most important commandment?" He said, "First, love God. Love him with all your heart, soul, and mind. The second is like it: Love your neighbor as yourself."

adapted from Matthew 22:36-39

Prayer

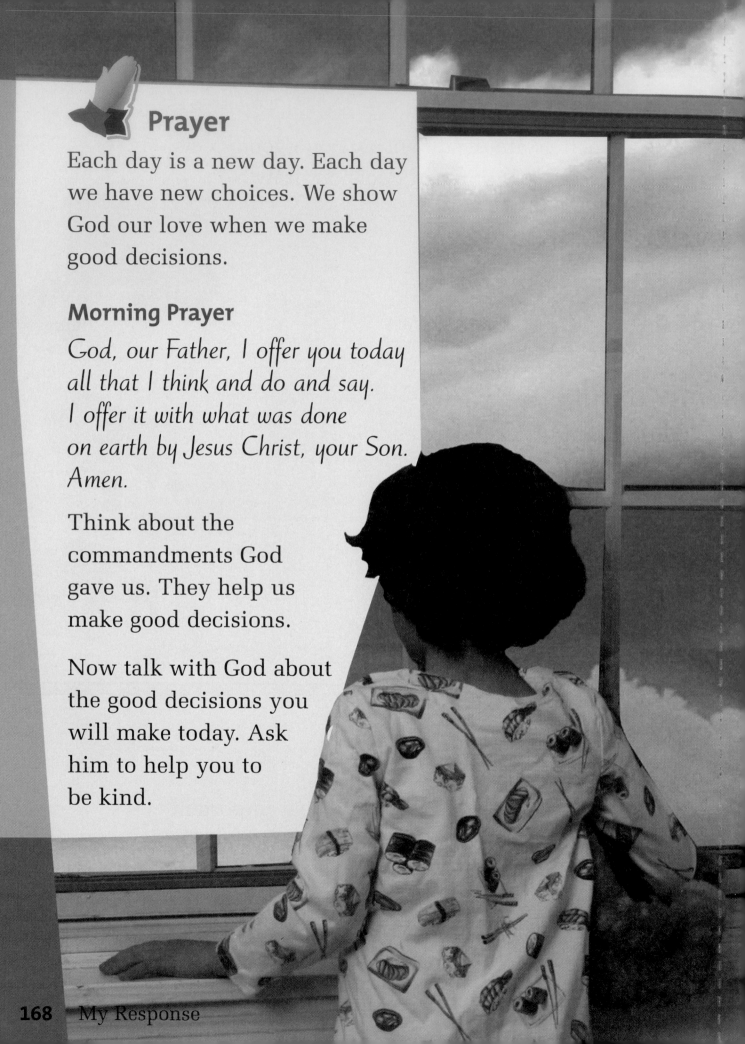

Each day is a new day. Each day we have new choices. We show God our love when we make good decisions.

Morning Prayer

God, our Father, I offer you today
all that I think and do and say.
I offer it with what was done
on earth by Jesus Christ, your Son.
Amen.

Think about the commandments God gave us. They help us make good decisions.

Now talk with God about the good decisions you will make today. Ask him to help you to be kind.

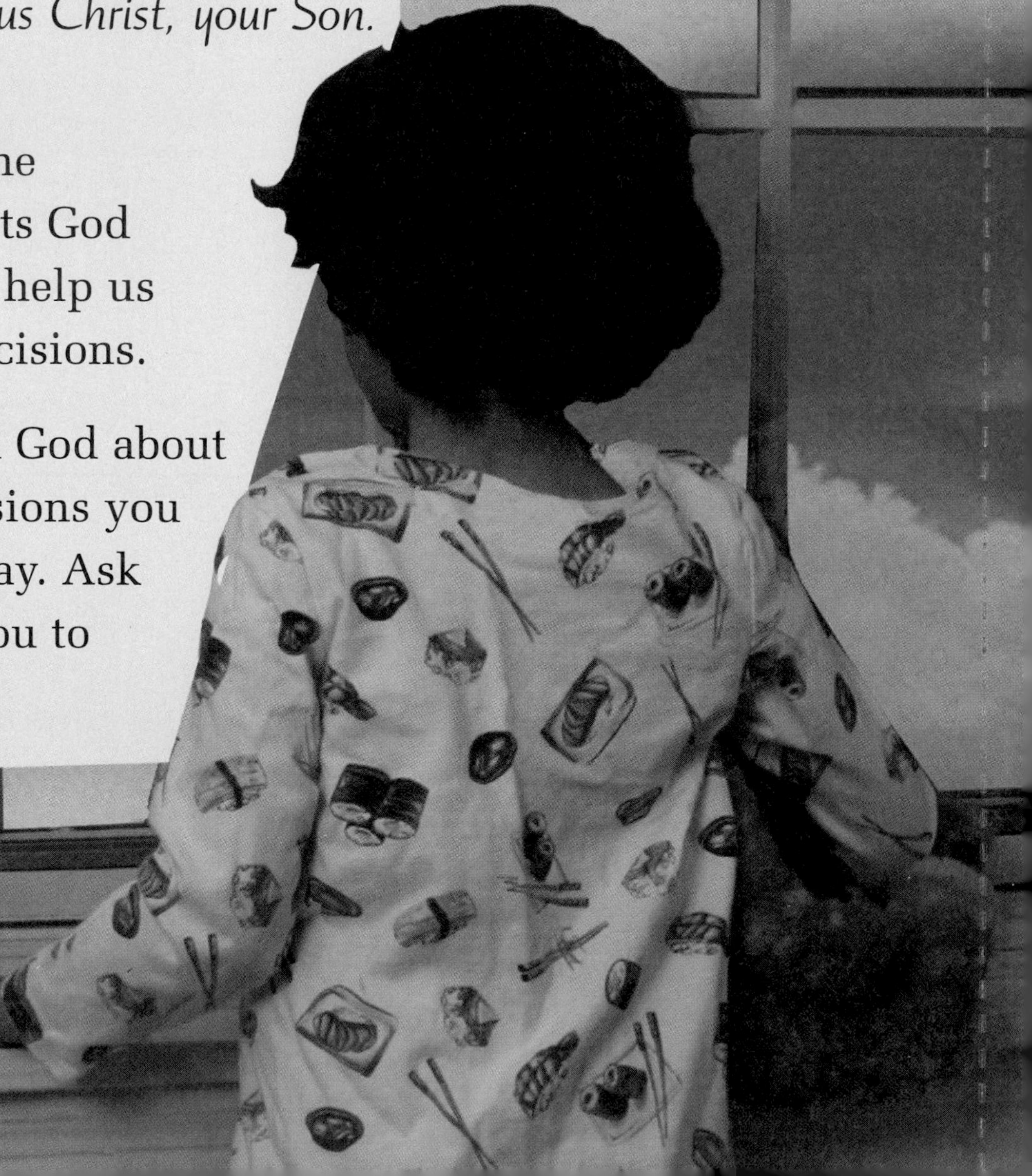

Living My Faith

Faith Summary

God gave us commandments.
They help us make good decisions.
Good decisions bring us peace.

Word I Learned

commandment

Ways of Being Like Jesus

Treat others as you would like to be treated.

With My Family

Show your love for your neighbors. Surprise them with flowers on their doorknobs.

Prayer

Jesus, my friend, thank you for helping me follow the commandments. I will try to make good decisions.

My Response

What good decision will you make?

RAISING FAITH-FILLED KIDS

a parent page

Focus on Faith

The Ten Commandments as Our Guide

Nighttime driving in a thunderstorm is frightening. Cloudbursts flood the streets. Keeping the car on the road is the only focus. The driver feels responsible for the passengers, especially the children sleeping in the back. Finally the family arrives home. Everyone hustles into the house, changes into dry clothing, and gathers for a short prayer of thanks to God. The relief the Hebrew people felt when they arrived at Mount Sinai was similar. They had escaped from Egypt and completed a difficult journey. When they stopped to thank God, he asked them whether they wanted to continue their relationship with him. They enthusiastically responded yes. God then gave them the Ten Commandments to guide their relationship with him and with one another.

Dinnertime Conversation Starter

Discuss with your child how each day is another step on the journey to God. Talk about how God is always present and how you as a parent will also be present to help or to answer questions. Explain how sound decisions can be made by following the Ten Commandments, and use some familiar situations as examples.

Hints for at Home

Create a Ten Family Rules Poster. Children are more likely to follow rules when they believe the rules are reasonable and logical. Have your child take part in making some family rules, and encourage discussion about why he or she believes those particular rules are important. Then, on a large piece of construction paper or poster board, list your family rules. These should be rules that can be followed easily by the entire family.

Spirituality in Action

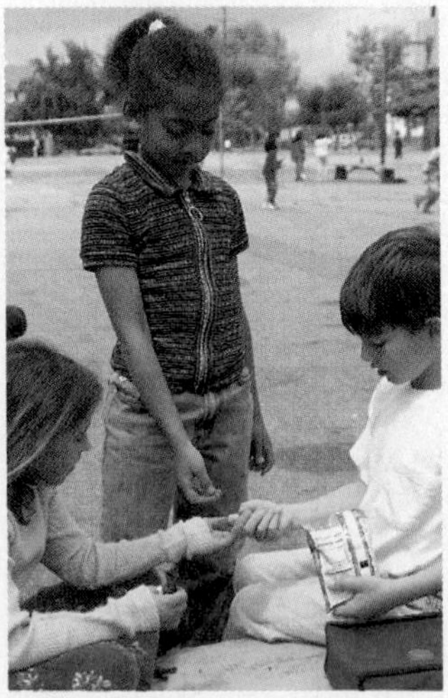

Good rules are those that are applied with consistency and fairness. Talk with your child about rules that we have in both the world and the home. Encourage discussion about how following rules contributes to peaceful living. Be sure to discuss the consequences of not following rules.

Focus on Prayer

Your child is learning the Morning Prayer. Mornings present perfect opportunities for your child to think about what types of choices he or she might face throughout the day. Say the Morning Prayer with your child as he or she is waking up, and then remind him or her that each day is a brand-new opportunity for us to do as God wants us to do. Visit www.FindingGod.org for words to the prayer.

Jesus Cares for Us

Session 22

Did you ever say something hurtful?

Did you ever take something that was not yours?

How did this make you feel?

How do you think it made the other person feel?

Prayer

Jesus, my helper, teach me how to care. Then I can help others.

A Lost Sheep

Jesus told a story.
He said,

Imagine you are a shepherd.
You have one hundred sheep.
One gets lost.

You leave all your sheep.
You go to look for the lost one.
You look everywhere.

Then you finally find it.
You are so happy!
You carry it home carefully.
You tell everyone you
found your lost sheep.

A person who does
something wrong is like
that lost sheep. All of heaven
is happy when that lost
sheep is found.

adapted from Luke 15:3-7

A Caring Shepherd

Jesus is like that shepherd. He will bring us back to him. He will do so as gently as a shepherd carries a little lamb.

Lost Sheep

Write the correct word on the line.

1. Jesus is like a __________.	**lost**
2. We are like his __________.	**shepherd**
3. He looks for us when we are __________.	**finds**
4. He always __________ us.	**sheep**

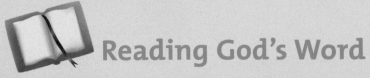

Reading God's Word

Jesus said, "I am the good shepherd."

John 10:11

God Always Forgives

When we choose to do something wrong, we **sin.** A sin can be something we do. A sin can be something we say.

Sins hurt our friendship with God and others.

When we are sorry, we ask God for **forgiveness.** God always forgives us. That is because God's love is greater than any sin.

I am sorry.
I like you.
I want to be your friend.
I will try to do better.
I apologize.
Please forgive me.

Did You Know?

When someone says, "I am sorry," we say, "I forgive you." Try it!

I forgive you.

Prayer

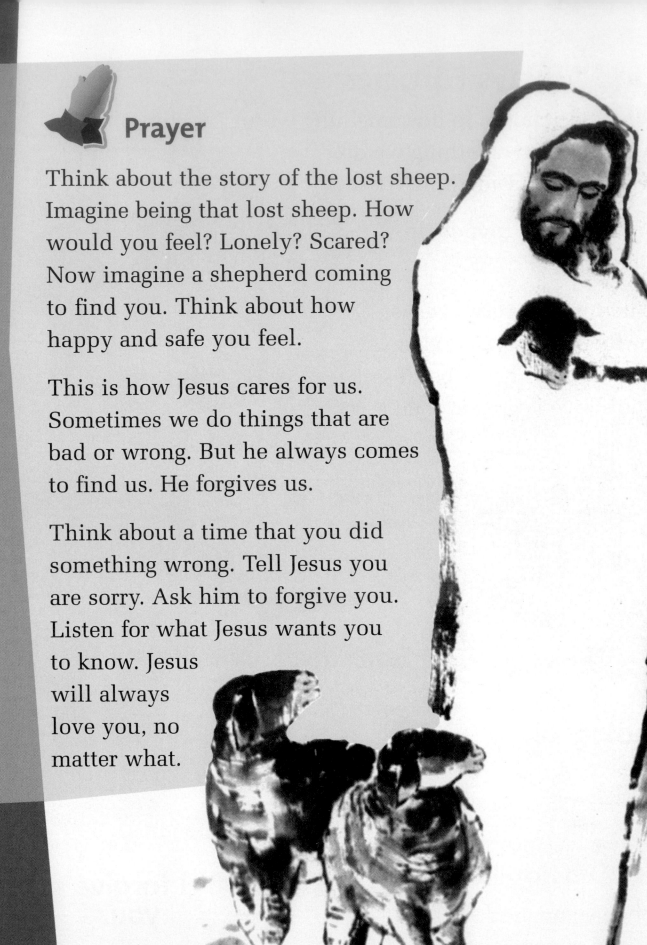

Think about the story of the lost sheep. Imagine being that lost sheep. How would you feel? Lonely? Scared? Now imagine a shepherd coming to find you. Think about how happy and safe you feel.

This is how Jesus cares for us. Sometimes we do things that are bad or wrong. But he always comes to find us. He forgives us.

Think about a time that you did something wrong. Tell Jesus you are sorry. Ask him to forgive you. Listen for what Jesus wants you to know. Jesus will always love you, no matter what.

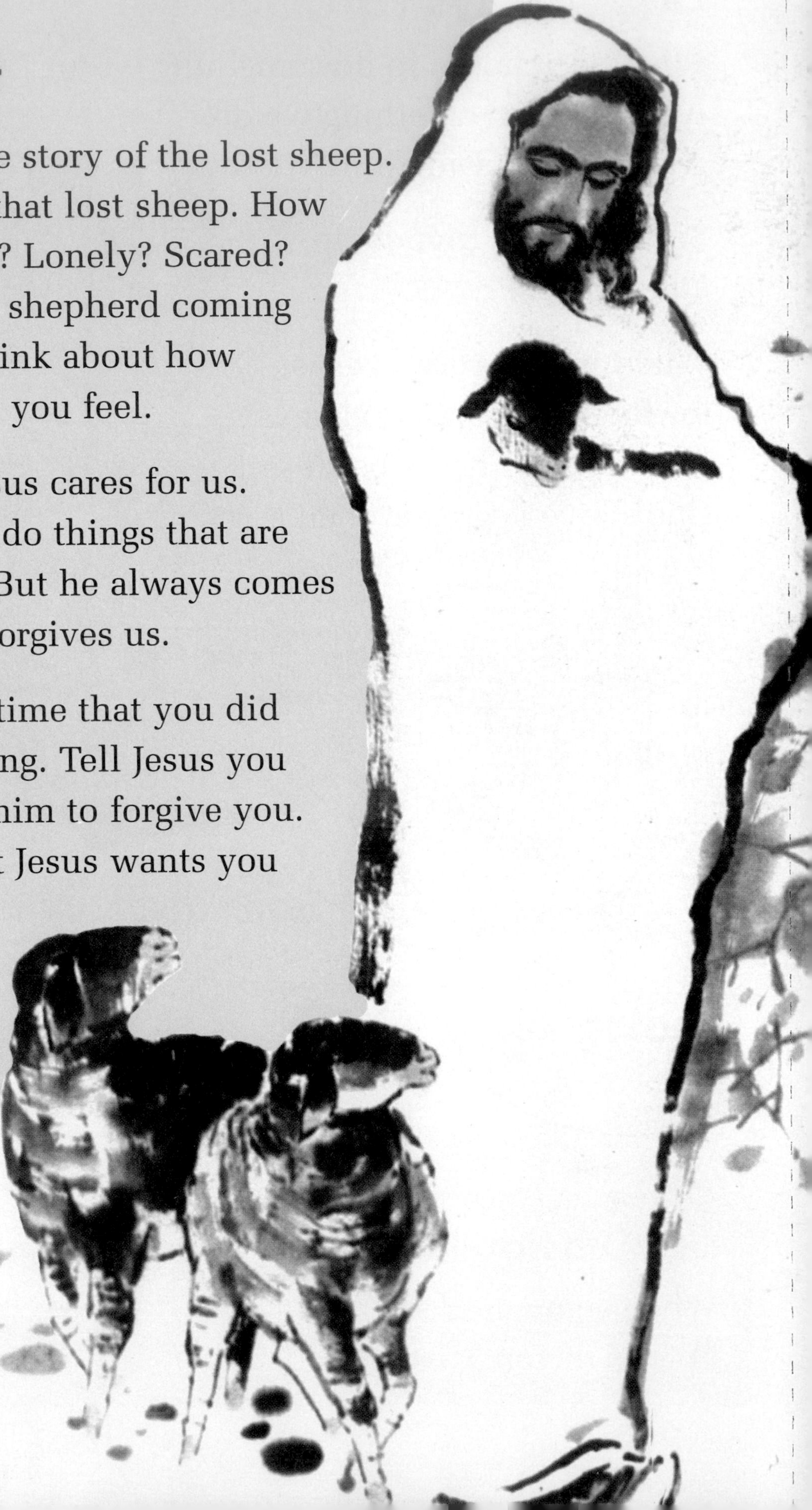

Living My Faith

Faith Summary

God's love is greater than any sin. When we feel bad for what we have done, we say we are sorry. God always forgives us.

Words I Learned

forgiveness **sin**

Ways of Being Like Jesus

When someone says, "I am sorry," say, "I forgive you."

With My Family

Talk about a time when someone forgave you. How did you feel?

Prayer

Jesus, thank you for teaching me about forgiveness. Help me to forgive others.

My Response

How will you show you are sorry when you have hurt someone?

Focus on Faith

Jesus, the Good Shepherd

In Jesus' time a shepherd had a hard, lonely life filled with danger. Jacob speaks about the long, cold nights he endured. David describes killing a lion and a bear that came to raid his flock. The threat of predatory animals, drought in the summer, and freezing rains in the winter was constant. The image of the Good Shepherd is that of someone who pays constant attention to the needs of the flock in spite of the danger. It is also the image of someone who is willing to risk everything to bring the one stray home. Jesus cares for each of us with that same constancy.

Dinnertime Conversation Starter

Ask your child to recall with you some times when you were aware of Jesus' loving care for your family.

Spirituality in Action

Letting go of hurt feelings is a practiced art. Try using this analogy with your child the next time you notice that he or she is angry with someone: "Being angry with someone is just like carrying a big rock. When you hold on to the bad feeling, it makes you heavy in your heart. It weighs you down. But what would happen if you just opened up your hand and let the angry feeling go, like dropping the big rock?" Mention that Jesus is always ready to take us by the hand. As we hold on to him, he will help us forgive.

Focus on Prayer

Your child is learning the story about Jesus, the Good Shepherd, which illustrates his caring for us. Invite your child to share the story with you, while encouraging discussion about how it relates to his or her own life. Pause silently for a few moments, and think about how Jesus always rescues us if we stray.

Hints for at Home

Make apologizing and forgiveness important in your family. Parents, especially, should find opportunities to model good behavior. Talk with your child about what it means to apologize, and explain that in apologizing we are asking for forgiveness. Together list what we say when we apologize:

I am sorry.
I apologize.
I am sorry I hurt you.
Will you forgive me?
It is my fault.

Jesus Loves Families

Session 23

What are some things your parents ask you to do? Is it ever hard to obey them?

Prayer

Jesus, Son of God, show me how to love and obey my parents.

Jesus Obeyed His Parents

Jesus and his parents were at a great celebration. On the way home, Mary and Joseph found out Jesus was not with them. They were so worried! So they rushed back.

Mary and Joseph looked for Jesus. Finally they found him. Mary said to him, “We have been so worried about you.”

Mary and Joseph told Jesus, “Now come home with us.” Jesus did as his parents said.

adapted from Luke 2:41-51

A Special Gift

God gave your parents a gift.
He gave them *you*.

You were everything they had hoped for. They were so happy. So they took good care of you. They made sure you were warm. They made sure you were fed. They taught you about God.

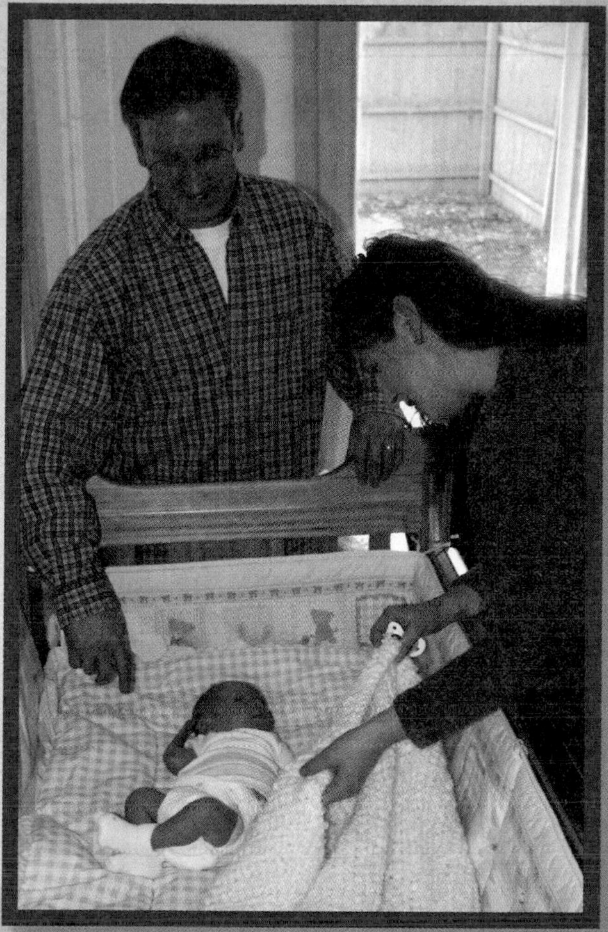

Now you are older. Your parents care about you more than ever before. They want you to be happy. They want you to be healthy. They want the best for you.

When you listen to your parents, God is happy. When you love your parents, God is happy.

Did You Know?

"Obey your parents" is a commandment. Jesus followed this commandment.

Make Your Parents Happy

How can you make your parents happy?
Circle the words in the puzzle.

honor **love** **obey** **help**

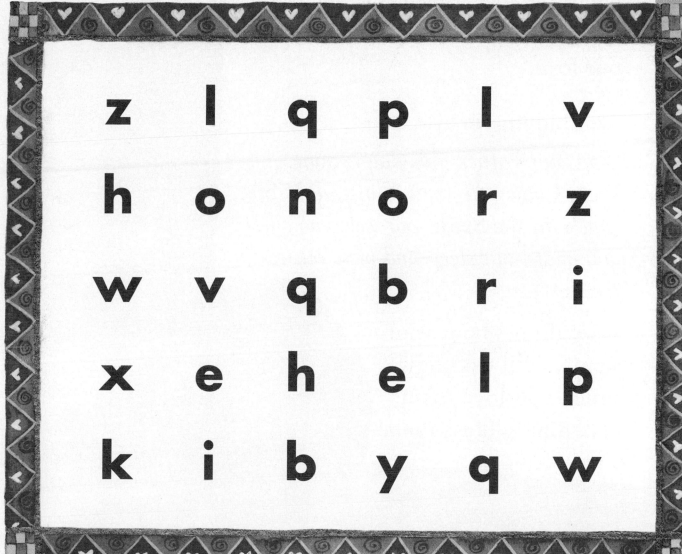

z	l	q	p	l	v
h	o	n	o	r	z
w	v	q	b	r	i
x	e	h	e	l	p
k	i	b	y	q	w

Reading God's Word

Love your mother and father. Obey them. Help them. Then you will have a long and happy life.

adapted from Exodus 20:12

Prayer

At the end of each day, we think about what we have done. We think about the decisions we made. We think about how we showed God our love.

Evening Prayer

God, our Father, this day is done.
We ask you and Jesus Christ, your Son,
that with the Spirit, our welcome guest,
you guard our sleep and bless our rest.
Amen.

Now think about your family. Tell God how much you love them. Ask him to bless them.

Living My Faith

Faith Summary

Jesus loved and obeyed his parents. God wants us to obey our parents too. When we show love for our parents, we show love for God.

Ways of Being Like Jesus

Do what your parents ask without complaining or arguing.

With My Family

Talk with your parents about when they were young. What kinds of rules did they have to obey?

Prayer

Jesus, Son of God, thank you for teaching me to obey and care for my parents.

My Response

How will you ask God to bless your parents?

RAISING FAITH-FILLED KIDS

a parent page

Focus on Faith

Honoring Our Parents

It is tempting to interpret the commandment that tells children to honor their parents as a call for instant obedience. In biblical times honoring one's parents meant respecting them as sources of wisdom and making a commitment to care for them in their old age. We, as sons and daughters ourselves, are the most influential example of what it means to respect parents. Especially now, while our children are in their formative years, we are teaching them the fundamental attitudes they will act out in their behavior toward us as they get older.

Dinnertime Conversation Starter

Share with your family your favorite memories of your parents, your children's grandparents. Discuss ways your family can make life easier and more enjoyable for older relatives.

Hints for at Home

One simple and fun way to teach children that they belong to part of a larger community is by creating a family tree. A family tree is a great visual teaching tool that allows children to learn about the relationships they share with other family members, while also strengthening personal and family identities. With your child, create a tree, and adorn it with drawings or photographs of people in your family. Be sure to share interesting stories and funny memories about each family member.

Focus on Prayer

Your child has learned a simple version of the Evening Prayer, to be said before bedtime each night. Set aside some special time to say the prayer together and talk peacefully and quietly about one another's day. Visit www.FindingGod.org for the words to the prayer.

Our Catholic Heritage

Early Christian Celts were deeply spiritual people and took time to craft prayers for many of life's activities. Following is a traditional Celtic bedtime prayer, written in Scotland long ago:

I Lie Down This Night

I lie down this night with God,
And God will lie down with me;
I lie down this night with Christ,
And Christ will lie down with me;
I lie down this night with the Spirit,
And the Spirit will lie down with me;
God and Christ and the Spirit
Be lying down with me.

from *Carmina Gadelica*

God Loves the World

Session
24

What do all these things have in common?

Prayer

Jesus, help me take care of God's world.
Then I can show my love for all of creation.

The First Garden

God took the first man to a beautiful garden. He asked the man to take care of it. Then God created different animals and birds. God said to the man, "Give them names." So, the man gave names to the animals. And he gave names to the birds.

adapted from Genesis 2:15,19-20

Reading God's Word

The land gives us food and flowers.
Our God blesses us.

adapted from Psalm 67:7

Caring for Our World

God made our world. That is why it is beautiful. We help keep it beautiful. We take care of the animals and plants. We do this for ourselves. We do this for our neighbors. And we do this for God.

Did You Know?

Forests are special places. They give animals homes. They keep our air clean. They even give us important medicines.

Caring for God's Creatures

Matt and Kara were playing. Matt saw something move. "What is it?" asked Matt. They ran over. It was a small, scared turtle. They told Mom and Dad.

Kara asked, "Can we keep it?"

"No," said Dad. Dad was an animal doctor. He knew all about turtles. This was a healthy turtle. This kind belonged in the wild. "God made special homes for these turtles. We have to care for God's world."

Matt said, "We can care for the turtle. We can return it to its home." So Dad took it to a nearby pond. He put it gently in the grass.

Then another turtle came over. Plop! Both turtles went into the water. They swam away together.

Everyone smiled.
"God's world is a
beautiful place," said Dad.

What Can You Do?

How will you care for God's world? Draw a picture and write a sentence.

____

____

Prayer

Imagine you are outside. It is your favorite kind of day. Maybe you see clouds. Maybe you feel a gentle breeze. Look around. Maybe you see your favorite animals too. You can see all of your favorite things that God created.

God loves us. He fills our lives with beautiful things. Thank him for these things. Tell him how you will care for them. Listen in your heart to what God wants you to know.

Living My Faith

Faith Summary

God made a beautiful world. He wants us to care for plants and animals. We take care of them for ourselves and others.

Ways of Being Like Jesus

Care for God's world. Be kind to every living thing.

With My Family

Talk with your family about making your porch or yard animal-friendly. Can you hang a bird house?

Prayer

Thank you, God, for this beautiful world.
I will care for the wonderful things you have given me.

My Response

How will you show God your love for animals?

Focus on Faith

Caring for Our World

A man was told that he had inoperable cancer and had only a few months to live. He decided to spend the time he had left cleaning up the stream in the back of his property. Now, a number of years later, he is still alive. Salmon are once again swimming in the stream. His small decision had great benefits both for the ecology of the world and for himself. The small decisions that we make today regarding whether to care for the environment will have a great impact on the lives of our children in the years to come. They will inherit the world that we create for them.

Dinnertime Conversation Starter

With your family examine how you are creating a better environment for the future. What more can your family do in the way of recycling or saving natural resources? How can you protect and show respect for animals?

Spirituality in Action

There are many ways, large and small, that your family can contribute to animal shelters. Shelters are always grateful for cash donations, but they are also happy to receive donations of paper towels, dog and cat food, litter, and cleaning supplies. In addition, volunteer opportunities are available, ranging from cleaning cages to walking dogs. Contact your local shelter for more information on ways you and your family can help, or visit **www.saveourstrays.com** to locate no-kill shelters.

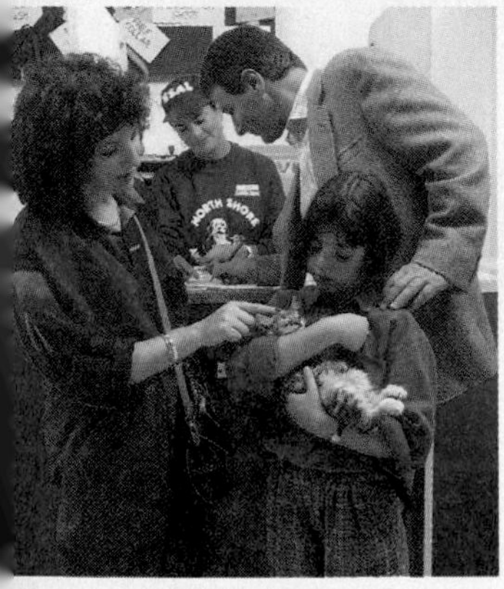

Hints for at Home

With your child create a bird feeder, birdbath, or butterfly feeder, and place it in a conspicuous area of your yard, where it will encourage God's creatures to seek out your home as a safe refuge. Talk with your child about how every animal and insect contributes to our world in its own special way and how by caring for living things, we show our love for God and his world. You may also want to visit the Humane Society of the United States at **www.hsus.org**, an organization that promotes respect and care for animals of all kinds.

Focus on Prayer

Over the year your child has learned the following prayers: Sign of the Cross, Glory Be to the Father, Lord's Prayer, Hail Mary, Prayer Before Meals, Prayer After Meals, as well as simple versions of a Morning Prayer and an Evening Prayer. Review them regularly so that he or she will remember them clearly next year. The exact words for each of the prayers can be found at www.FindingGod.org.

Review

Session 25

Saint Ignatius always showed his love for God. He prayed to God. He cared for other people. He followed God's two great commandments.

Love God. Love your neighbor.

Prayer

Jesus, my guide, help me be like Saint Ignatius.
I will love God and my neighbor.

Faith Summary

God gave us commandments.
They help us make good decisions.
When we follow them, we are at
peace with God and others.

We all sin. God's love is greater
than any sin. He always forgives us.

Jesus is like the Good Shepherd.
He watches over us.

God wants us to obey our parents.
When we do, we obey God.

God made a beautiful world.
He wants us to take care of it.

I know God always loves

________________.

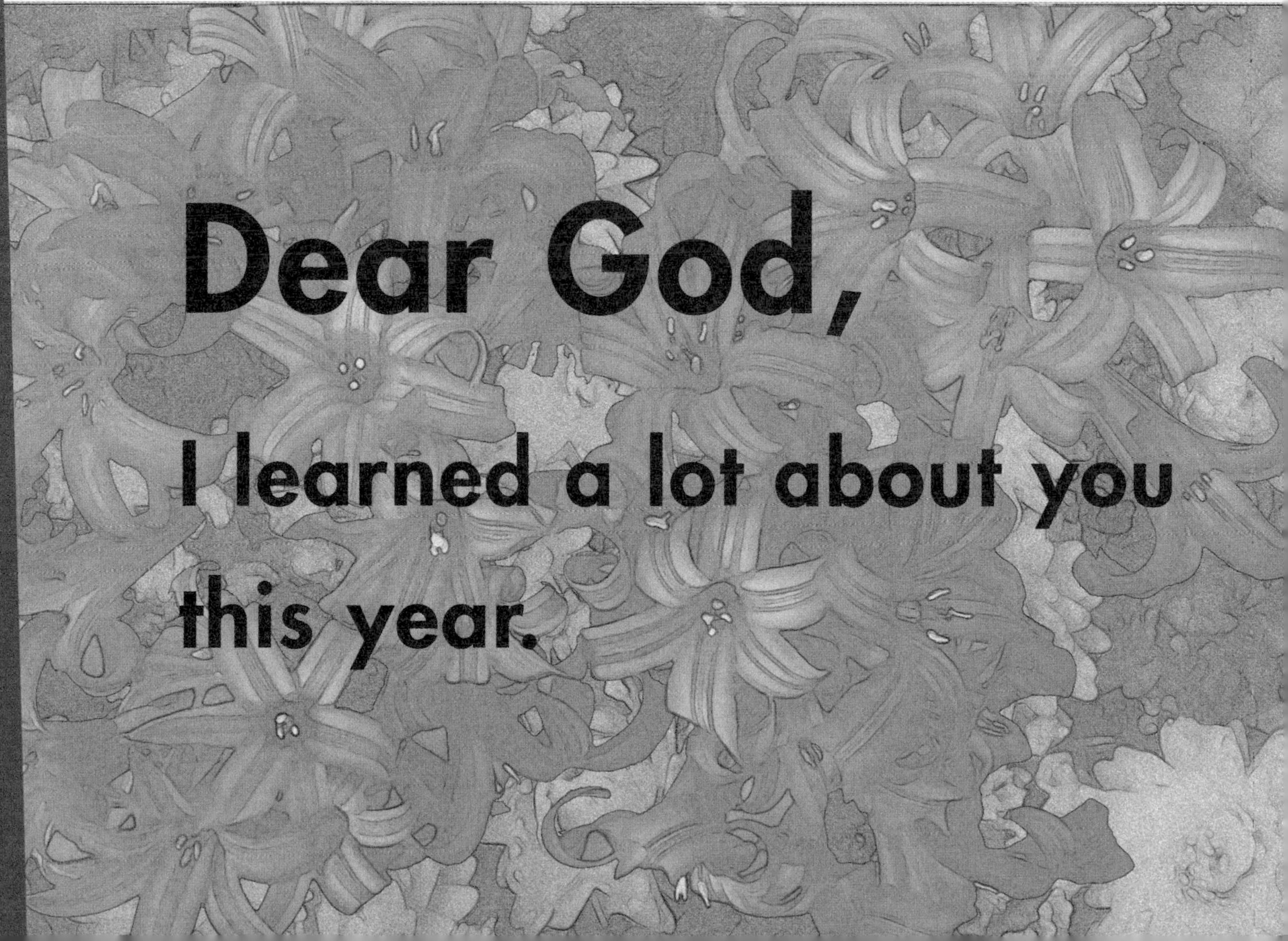

Dear God,

I learned a lot about you this year.

I learned that
you made plants,
animals, and the sea.

You made my family, friends, and me.

You sent Jesus as my guide.

I will always love Jesus
and know he is by my side.

Thank you,

____

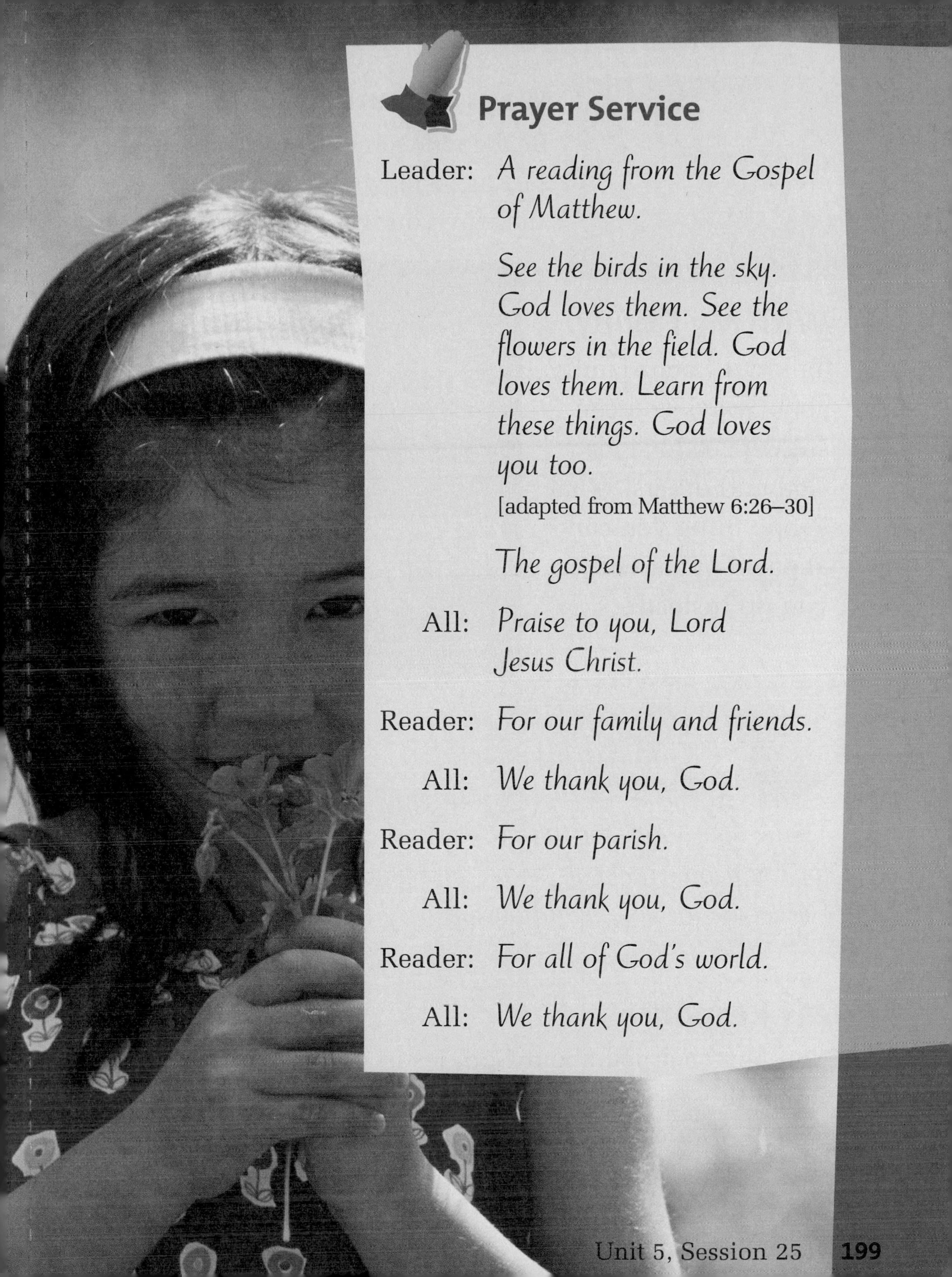

Prayer Service

Leader: *A reading from the Gospel of Matthew.*

See the birds in the sky. God loves them. See the flowers in the field. God loves them. Learn from these things. God loves you too.

[adapted from Matthew 6:26–30]

The gospel of the Lord.

All: *Praise to you, Lord Jesus Christ.*

Reader: *For our family and friends.*

All: *We thank you, God.*

Reader: *For our parish.*

All: *We thank you, God.*

Reader: *For all of God's world.*

All: *We thank you, God.*

Living My Faith

Ways of Being Like Jesus

Be a good example to others, just as Jesus was. Treat others the way you want to be treated.

With My Family

Talk with your family about ways you can show your love for God and others. What is one thing you can change? What will you do instead?

Prayer

Thank you, God, for this great world. Thank you for the people, animals, birds, and plants around me. I will care for your world always.

My Response

You have learned about God, Jesus, and the Holy Spirit this year. How will you show your love for God? For others? For his great world?

The Year in Our Church

Liturgical Calendar

The liturgical calendar shows us the feasts and seasons of the Church year.

Liturgical Year

We get ready to welcome Jesus during **Advent.**

Christmas celebrates the time when Jesus was born.

Lent is the time before Easter. It is a time to do good things.

Holy Week is the week before Easter. We remember that Jesus died for us.

On **Easter** Jesus rose from the dead.

On **Pentecost** the Holy Spirit came to Jesus' friends.

All Saints Day is the day we remember everyone in heaven.

Ordinary Time is time set aside for everyday living. We live as followers of Jesus.

Advent

Mary and Joseph waited for Jesus to be born.

We wait to celebrate Jesus' birth. We call this wait Advent.

Prayer

God, help me be patient as I prepare for Christmas.

Waiting for Jesus

Jesus was about to be born. Mary and Joseph were getting ready for him.

But their ruler wanted to count all his people. So Mary and Joseph went to be counted. They had to go far from home. They had nowhere to rest. So they stayed in a stable. They waited there for Jesus to be born.

adapted from Luke 2:1-7

What Did Mary and Joseph Do?

Unscramble these letters.
Then write them in the blanks.

w t a i d e

Mary and Joseph __ __ __ __ __ __ for Jesus.

The Advent Wreath

Did you ever have to wait for something?

Sometimes it is hard to wait. But our wait can be worth it!

The Advent wreath reminds us we are waiting to celebrate the birth of Jesus. It reminds us he is coming.

The wreath has four candles. We light a candle each week. Each lit candle means Christmas is getting closer.

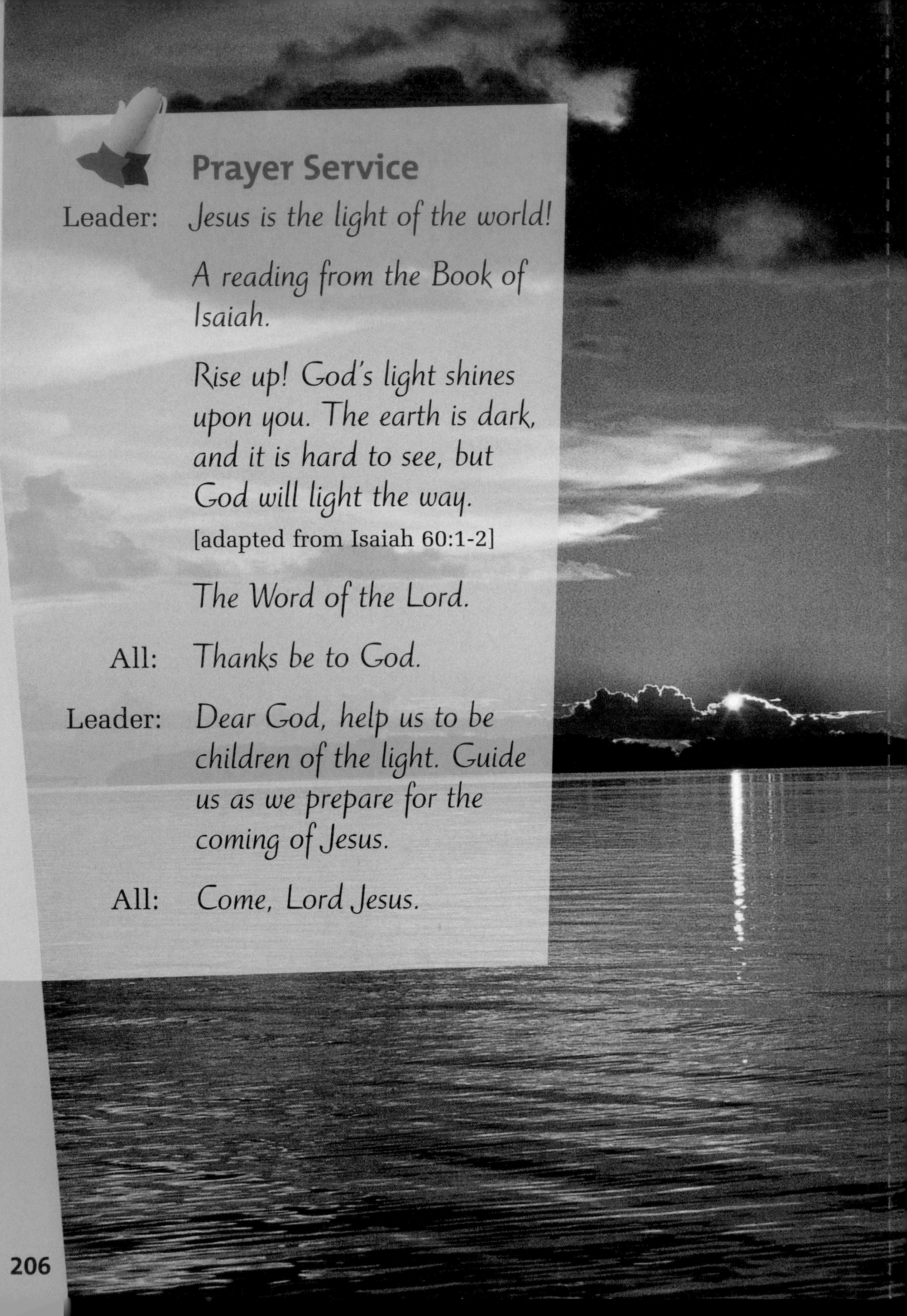

Prayer Service

Leader: *Jesus is the light of the world!*

A reading from the Book of Isaiah.

Rise up! God's light shines upon you. The earth is dark, and it is hard to see, but God will light the way.

[adapted from Isaiah 60:1-2]

The Word of the Lord.

All: *Thanks be to God.*

Leader: *Dear God, help us to be children of the light. Guide us as we prepare for the coming of Jesus.*

All: *Come, Lord Jesus.*

Christmas

Shepherds were watching their sheep.
An angel came to them. They were afraid.
The angel said, "Do not be afraid. I have good news. Jesus has been born."

Then more angels came. They said,
"Glory to God. Peace on earth."

adapted from Luke 2:8-14

Prayer

Thank you, God, for sending us your Son, Jesus.

Looking for Jesus

The shepherds were very happy.
They went to find Jesus.

adapted from Luke 2:15

God's Gift to Everyone

God sent Jesus to Mary and Joseph.
God sent Jesus to the shepherds.
God sent Jesus to us.
Jesus is a gift to us all.

Good News

The shepherds heard the good news. Jesus, the Prince of Peace, was born. We can be like Jesus. We can help one another live in peace.

Jesus Is Born

Help the shepherds find Jesus. Draw a line.

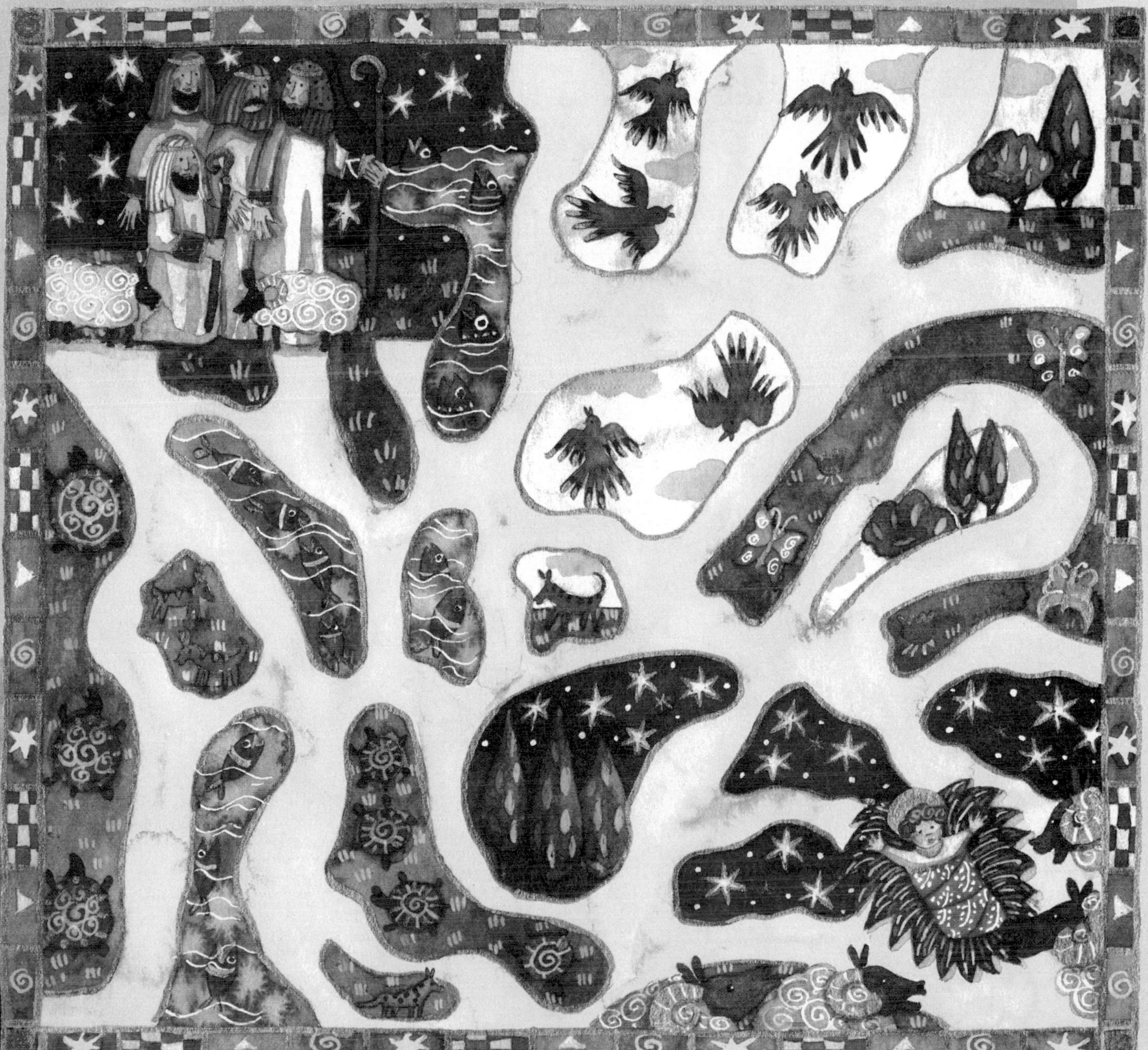

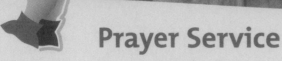

Prayer Service

Leader: *Peace be with you.*

All: *And also with you.*

Leader: *We celebrate the good news of Jesus' birth. Let us welcome him into our lives. Let us live in peace together.*

A reading from the Book of Isaiah.

A child is born for us. A son is given to us. They call him Mighty God. They call him Prince of Peace. He will rule in peace forever.

[adapted from Isaiah 9:5-6]

The Word of the Lord.

All: *Thanks be to God.*

Lent

This is a special time of year. We call it Lent.
It is a time to do good things.

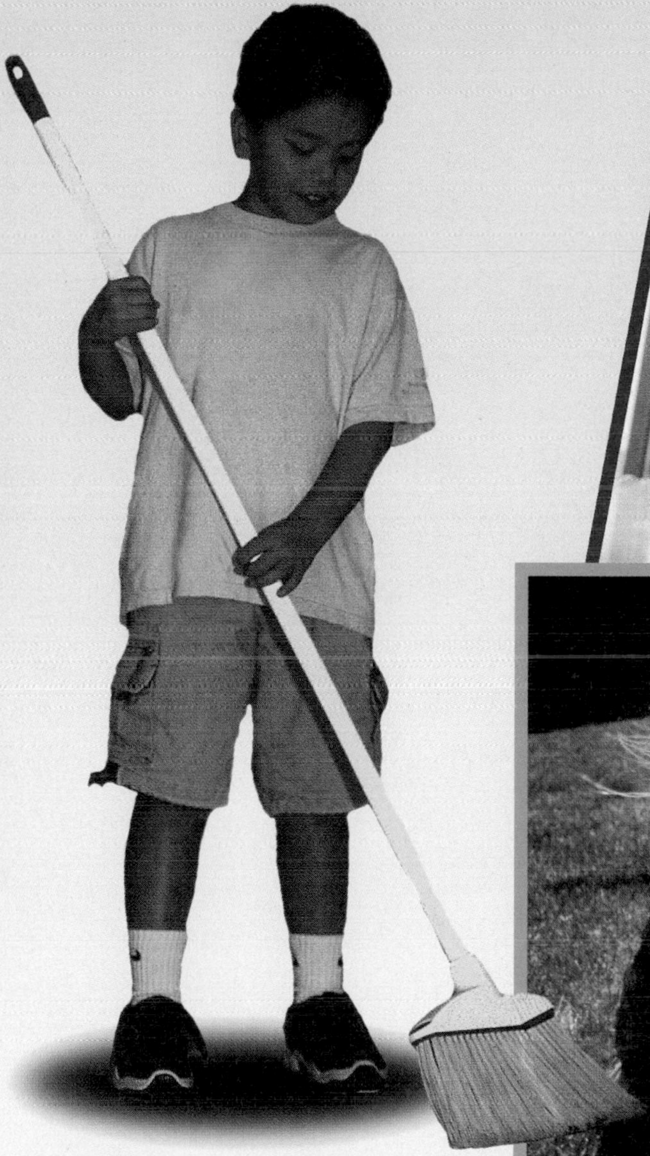

Prayer

Jesus, my guide, help me to do good things this Lent.
I want to stay close to God.

Grow With God

This tree grows near a stream. It is healthy. The water from the stream nourishes it. The water helps it grow strong.

We are like the healthy tree.
And God is like our stream.
When we are close to him,
we grow stronger and happier.
adapted from the Book of Psalms 1:3

We Grow With Good Deeds

During Lent, we make a special point to do good deeds. We try to be like Jesus. Then we can grow closer to God. What good deeds will you do during Lent?

I will
play fairly.
I will ____
____
____________.
I will _____
____
____________.

A Special Time

The first day of Lent is called Ash Wednesday. Ashes are placed on our foreheads. The ashes remind us that Lent is a special time.

Prayer Service

Leader: *Let us begin our prayer with the Sign of the Cross.*

We offer God our good deeds in this time of Lent. Let us pray that they will help us grow closer to God.

A reading from the Gospel of John.

I am the vine, and you are the branches. If you stay close to me and I to you, you will produce much fruit.
[adapted from John 15:5]

The gospel of the Lord.

All: *Praise to you, Lord Jesus Christ.*

Holy Week

During Holy Week, we think about how Jesus lived. He taught his friends to love others. How do you show others your love?

Prayer

Jesus, my teacher, help me show my love to others.
I want to be like you.

Jesus Teaches His Friends

Jesus loved his friends very much. He wanted them to know this. He decided to show them. So he put some water in a bowl. Then he washed his friends' feet.

Jesus said, "You say that I am your teacher. If I am, learn from me. I am your friend. If I wash your feet, you should wash the feet of others. Treat others as I treat you."

adapted from John 13:1-15

Love One Another

Jesus showed his friends how to love others. He wanted them to do as he did. Jesus wants us to follow his example too. When we help others, we are being like Jesus.

I Can Follow Jesus

You can follow in Jesus' footsteps.
You can show others your love.
What can you do?
Finish the sentence.

Prayer Service

Leader: *Jesus was sad to leave his friends. Before he left, he gave them a special message.*

A reading from the Gospel of John.

My children, I will be with you only a little while longer. Then I will be gone. I give you a new commandment: love one another. You should love one another as I have loved you. Then everyone will know you are my friends.

[adapted from John 13:33-35]

The gospel of the Lord.

All: *Praise to you, Lord Jesus Christ.*

Leader: *Let us always remember to walk in the footsteps of Jesus.*

All: *In the name of the Father,*
and of the Son,
and of the Holy Spirit.
Amen.

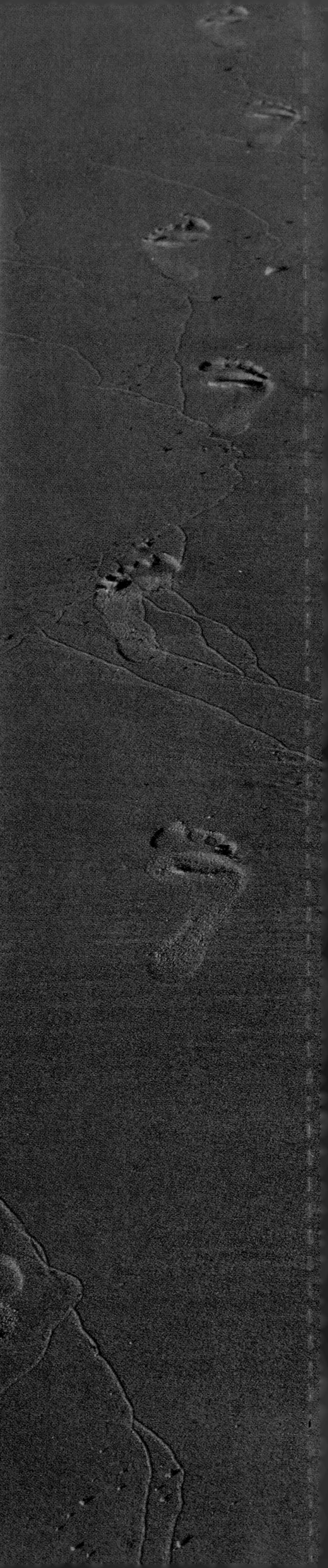

Easter

Easter is a happy time. We celebrate Jesus' rising from the dead. His Resurrection fills us with joy.

Prayer

Jesus, my friend, help me follow you.
I want to be with you someday.

Looking for Jesus

Jesus had died. Some women visited his tomb. They saw that the stone was rolled back. The tomb was empty! Then two angels came. They said, "Jesus is not here. He has been raised." The women were filled with joy. Jesus was alive! They ran to tell their friends.

adapted from Luke 24:1-9

Jesus Appeared to Many

On their way, the women saw Jesus. Many more people saw him too. After Jesus saw his friends, it was time to leave. He went to heaven. He went to be with his Father.

The Lord's Day

Why is Sunday special? It is the day we celebrate Jesus' Resurrection. We celebrate by going to Mass.

Celebrate Jesus

In what order did these happen? Use numbers.

The women tell their friends.

The women see angels.

The tomb is empty.

Women visit the tomb.

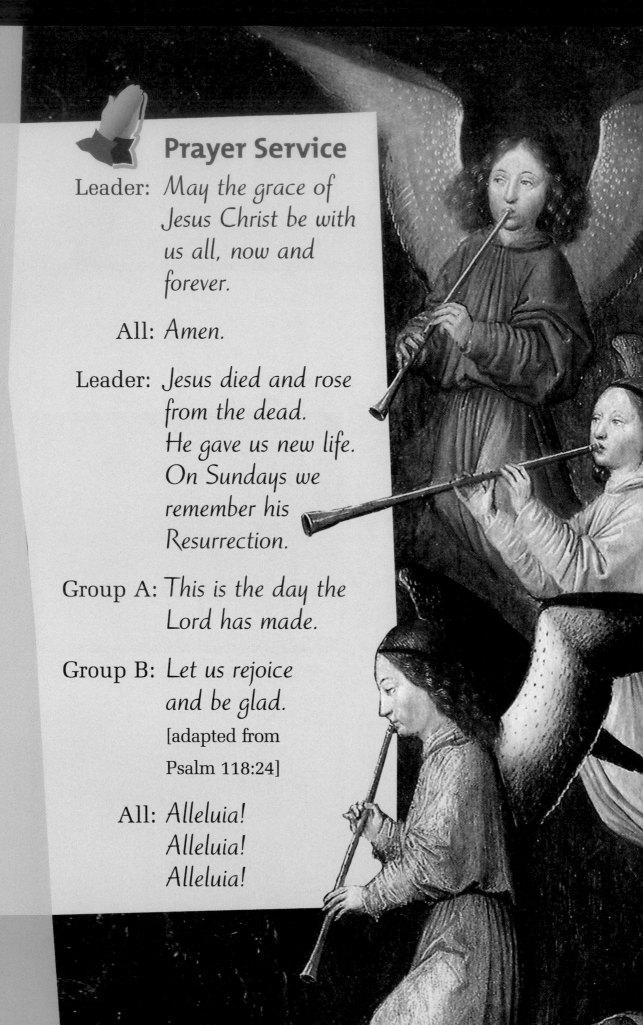

Prayer Service

Leader: *May the grace of Jesus Christ be with us all, now and forever.*

All: *Amen.*

Leader: *Jesus died and rose from the dead. He gave us new life. On Sundays we remember his Resurrection.*

Group A: *This is the day the Lord has made.*

Group B: *Let us rejoice and be glad.*
[adapted from Psalm 118:24]

All: *Alleluia!*
Alleluia!
Alleluia!

Pentecost

After Jesus rose from the dead, the Holy Spirit came. It was a time of joy. We call this special time Pentecost.

Prayer

Dear Jesus, give me the help of the Holy Spirit. He will help me tell others about you.

Sharing Jesus

Philip was a follower of Jesus. One day Philip went on a trip. On the road he met a man. The man wanted to learn about God.

The Holy Spirit was in Philip's heart. The Holy Spirit said to Philip, "Help the man. Teach the man." So Philip did. He told the man about Jesus.

The man was very happy. He asked Philip, "Will you baptize me?" The man wanted to become part of God's family.

adapted from Acts of the Apostles 8:26-38

The Holy Spirit Is With Us

The Holy Spirit was with Philip. The Holy Spirit is with all of us too. We can celebrate Pentecost every day. We can help others know Jesus. We can do this by telling them about him. The Holy Spirit will help us.

The Holy Spirit Is With Me

Show that the Holy Spirit is with you. Show how you can help someone. Draw a picture in the dove.

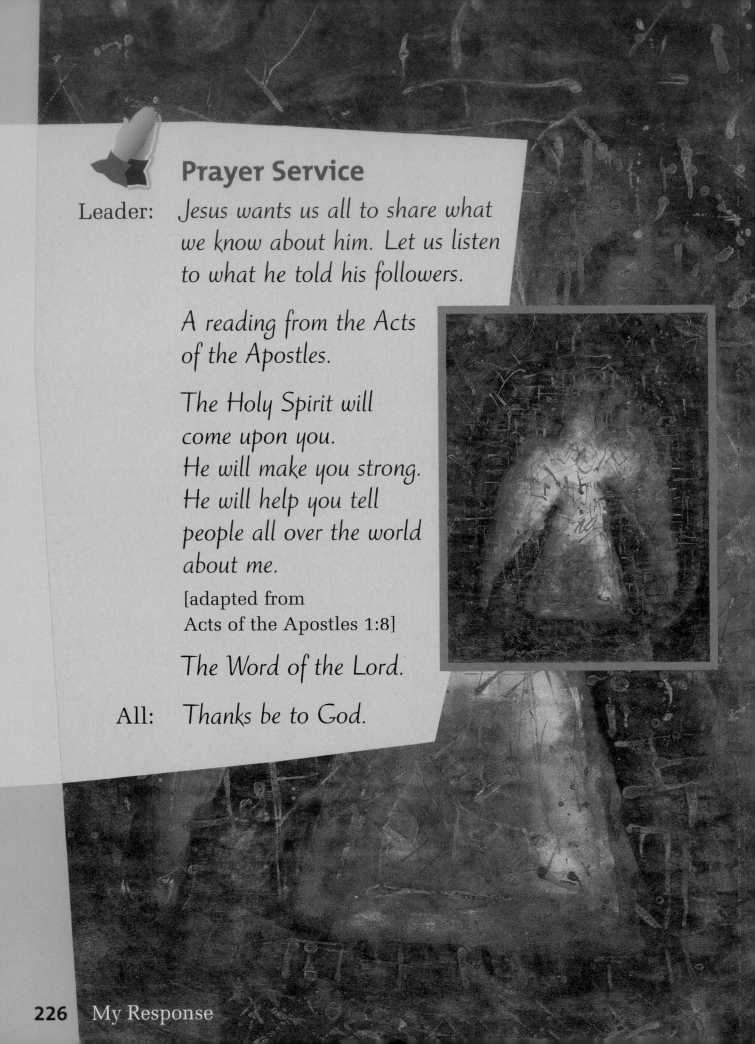

Prayer Service

Leader: *Jesus wants us all to share what we know about him. Let us listen to what he told his followers.*

A reading from the Acts of the Apostles.

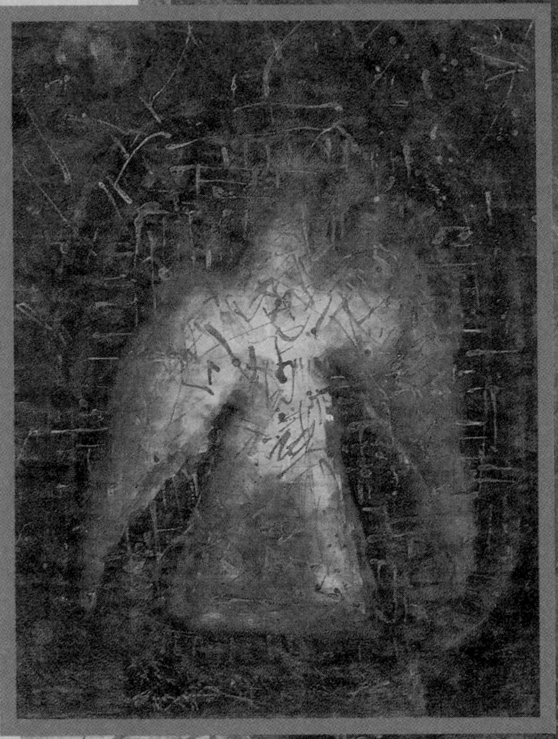

The Holy Spirit will
come upon you.
He will make you strong.
He will help you tell
people all over the world
about me.

[adapted from
Acts of the Apostles 1:8]

The Word of the Lord.

All: *Thanks be to God.*

All Saints Day

On All Saints Day, we think of everyone in heaven. They are with God. They are saints.

Prayer

Dear God, help me to be like the saints.
I want to love you as they did.

Children of God

Our Father loves us very much. We are called the children of God. One day we shall see him.

adapted from 1 John 3:1-2

Prayer Strips

Ask someone in heaven to pray for you. Put your prayer in a special place.

Dear ____________________, pray for me. Help me to ____________________ ____________________.

Dear ____________________, pray for me. Help me to ____________________ ____________________.

Dear ____________________, pray for me. Help me to ____________________ ____________________.

Dear ____________________, pray for me. Help me to ____________________ ____________________.

A Special Day

Think about your birthday. It is a day all for you. It is a day when people show how much they love you.

Saints have a special day too. We call it All Saints Day. On this day we show the saints our love. How? We think about them. We ask them to pray for us.

Saints Pray for Us

Saints are God's special friends. They are close to him. We ask them for their help. We ask them to talk to God for us. They ask him to watch over us. The saints ask God to care for us.

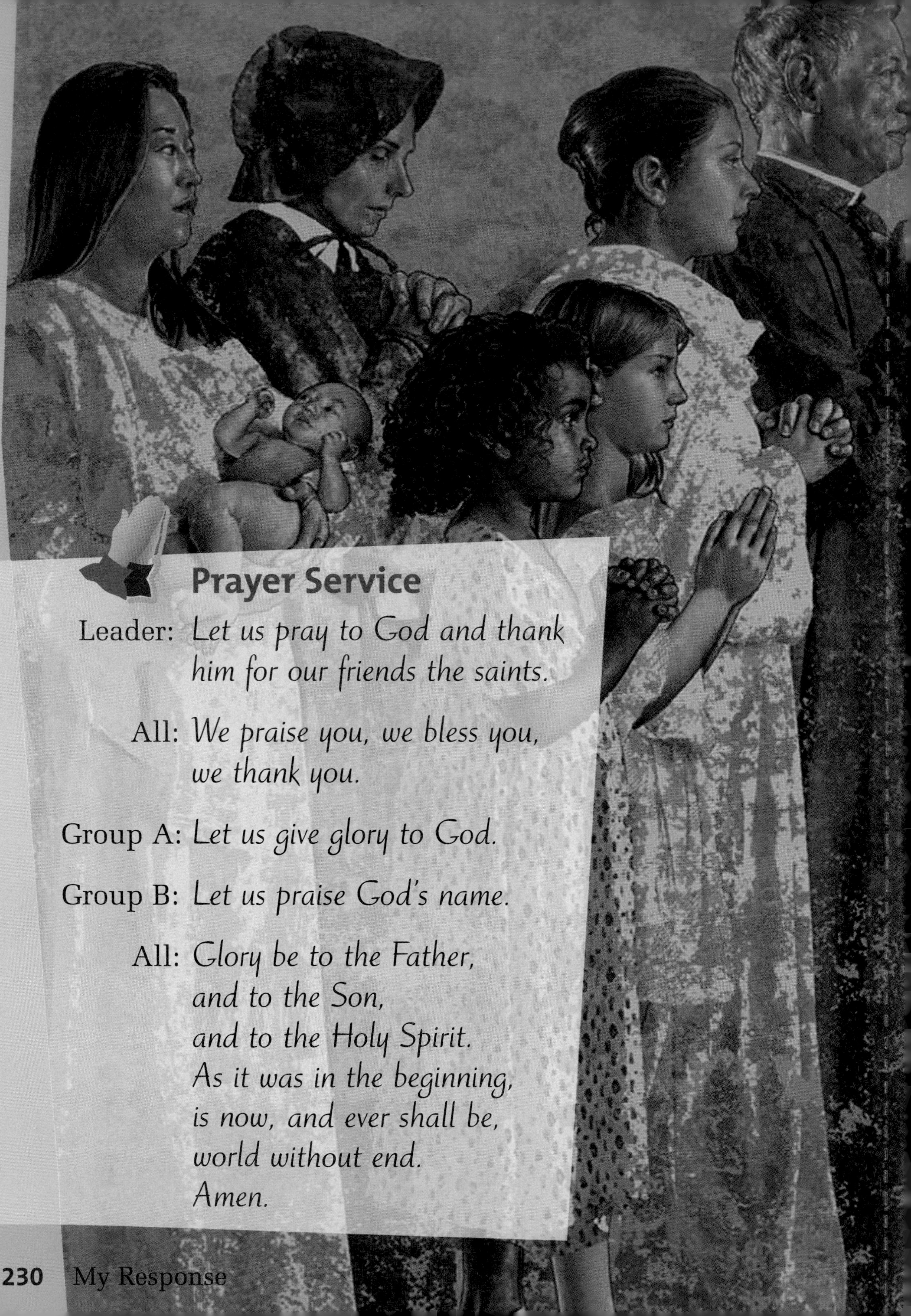

Prayer Service

Leader: *Let us pray to God and thank him for our friends the saints.*

All: *We praise you, we bless you, we thank you.*

Group A: *Let us give glory to God.*

Group B: *Let us praise God's name.*

All: *Glory be to the Father,*
and to the Son,
and to the Holy Spirit.
As it was in the beginning,
is now, and ever shall be,
world without end.
Amen.

Prayers and Practices of Our Faith

Grade 1

KNOWING AND PRAYING OUR FAITH

CELEBRATING OUR FAITH

LIVING OUR FAITH

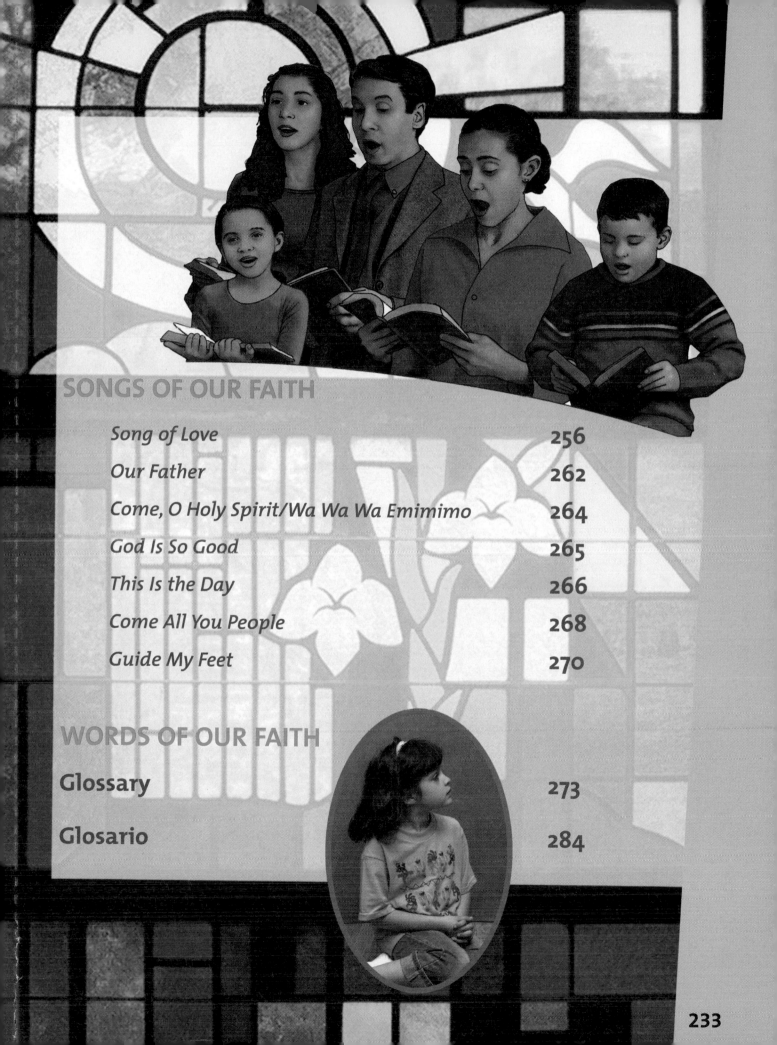

SONGS OF OUR FAITH

WORDS OF OUR FAITH

The Bible and You

God speaks to us in many ways. One way is through the Bible.

The Bible is God's message. The Bible is the story of God's promise to care for us. It teaches us about God's love for us.

The Bible teaches us about Jesus. Stories about Jesus are in the Gospels. We can learn about what Jesus said and did.

At Mass we hear stories from the Bible. We learn how we can share God's love with others.

The Bible has two parts. One part is the Old Testament. Another part is the New Testament. In the New Testament we learn about Jesus.

Prayer and How We Pray

Prayer is talking and listening to God.

God is everywhere. We can pray to God at any time and in any place.

God hears our prayers even when we pray silently. We can pray in our own words. We can learn prayers. Sometimes we can just be quiet and enjoy being with God.

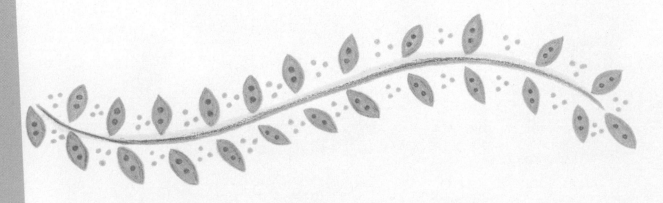

We pray to God often and in different ways. We can praise God. We can ask God for what we need. We can thank him. We can pray for ourselves and for others.

Sometimes we pray alone. Other times we pray with others.

Prayers to Take to Heart

It is good for us to know prayers by heart.

To learn prayers by heart means that we not only learn, or memorize, the words but also try to understand them and live them.

Sign of the Cross

In the name of the Father,

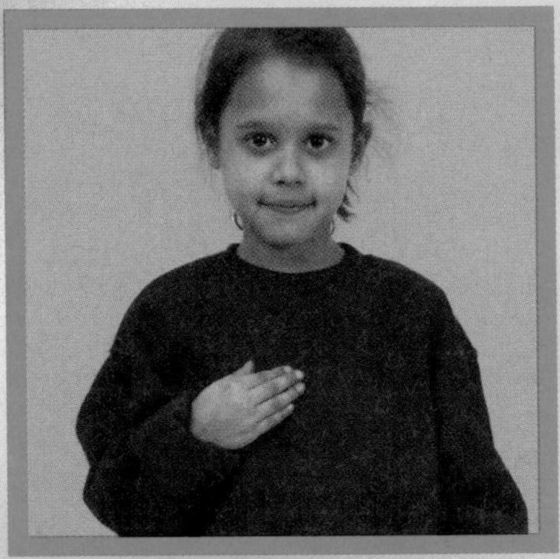

and of the Son,

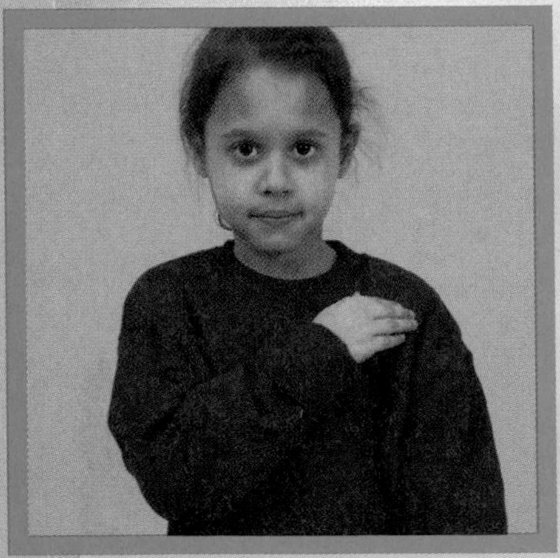

and of the Holy

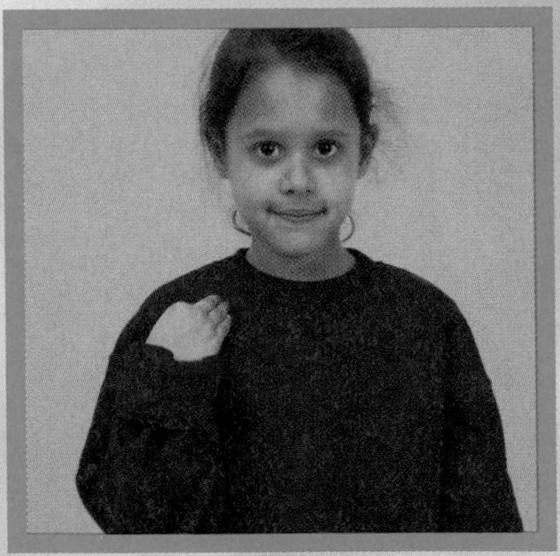

Spirit.

Amen.

Glory Be to the Father

Glory be to the Father,
and to the Son,
and to the Holy Spirit.
As it was in the beginning,
is now, and ever shall be,
world without end.
Amen.

Lord's Prayer

Our Father,
who art in heaven,
hallowed be thy name;
thy kingdom come;
thy will be done
on earth as it is in heaven.
Give us this day our daily bread;
and forgive us our trespasses
as we forgive those who trespass against us;
and lead us not into temptation,
but deliver us from evil.
Amen.

Hail Mary

Hail Mary, full of grace,
the Lord is with you.
Blessed are you among women,
and blessed is the fruit of your womb, Jesus.
Holy Mary, Mother of God,
pray for us sinners,
now and at the hour of our death.
Amen.

Guardian Angel Prayer

Angel of God, my guardian dear,
to whom God's love commits me here,
ever this day be at my side,
to light and guard, to rule and guide.
Amen.

Prayer for Vocations

God, thank you for loving me.
You have called me
to live as your child.
Help all your children
to love you and one another.
Amen.

Morning Prayer

God, our Father, I offer you today
all that I think and do and say.
I offer it with what was done
on earth by Jesus Christ, your Son.
Amen.

Evening Prayer

God, our Father, this day is done.
We ask you and Jesus Christ, your Son,
that with the Spirit, our welcome guest,
you guard our sleep and bless our rest.
Amen.

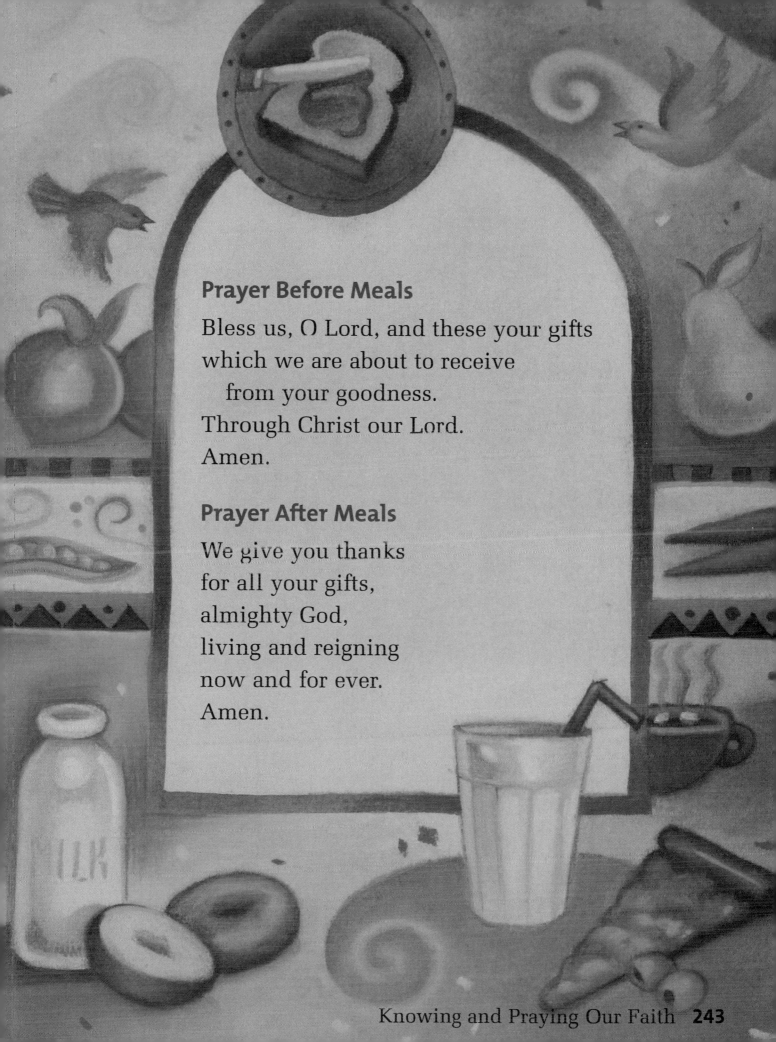

Prayer Before Meals

Bless us, O Lord, and these your gifts
which we are about to receive
from your goodness.
Through Christ our Lord.
Amen.

Prayer After Meals

We give you thanks
for all your gifts,
almighty God,
living and reigning
now and for ever.
Amen.

The Seven Sacraments

A sacrament is a special sign. Sacraments give us grace. They show us that Jesus loves us.

Sacraments help us to live the way God wants us to live. Sacraments are celebrated with us by priests.

Baptism

Baptism is the first sacrament we receive. At Baptism a priest pours blessed water on us. We become part of God's family, the Church.

Confirmation

At Confirmation the Holy Spirit makes us stronger in faith. The Holy Spirit helps us become better Christians.

Eucharist

At Mass the bread and wine become Jesus' Body and Blood. The Eucharist is a special meal that Jesus shares with us.

Penance

In Penance we celebrate God's forgiveness. We say we are sorry for our sins. The priest tells us that God forgives us.

Anointing of the Sick

The Anointing of the Sick brings Jesus' strength to people who are sick.

Holy Orders

Some men are called to be deacons, priests, or bishops. They receive the Sacrament of Holy Orders. They do Jesus' work in a special way.

Matrimony

Some men and women are called to be married. They promise to be faithful to each other for life. They share God's love with their children.

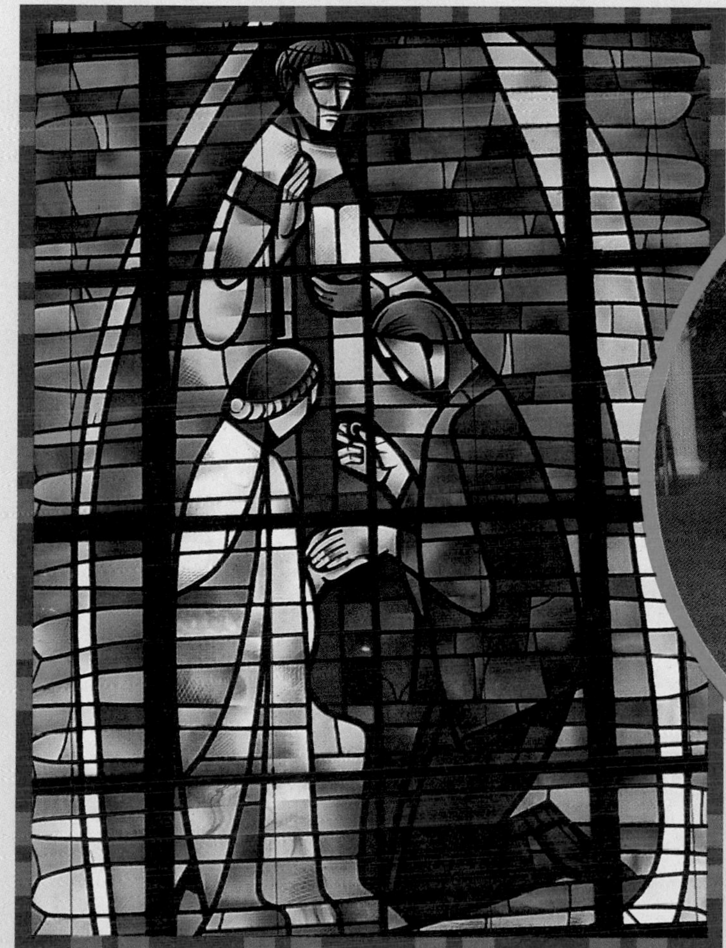

People and Things I See at Mass

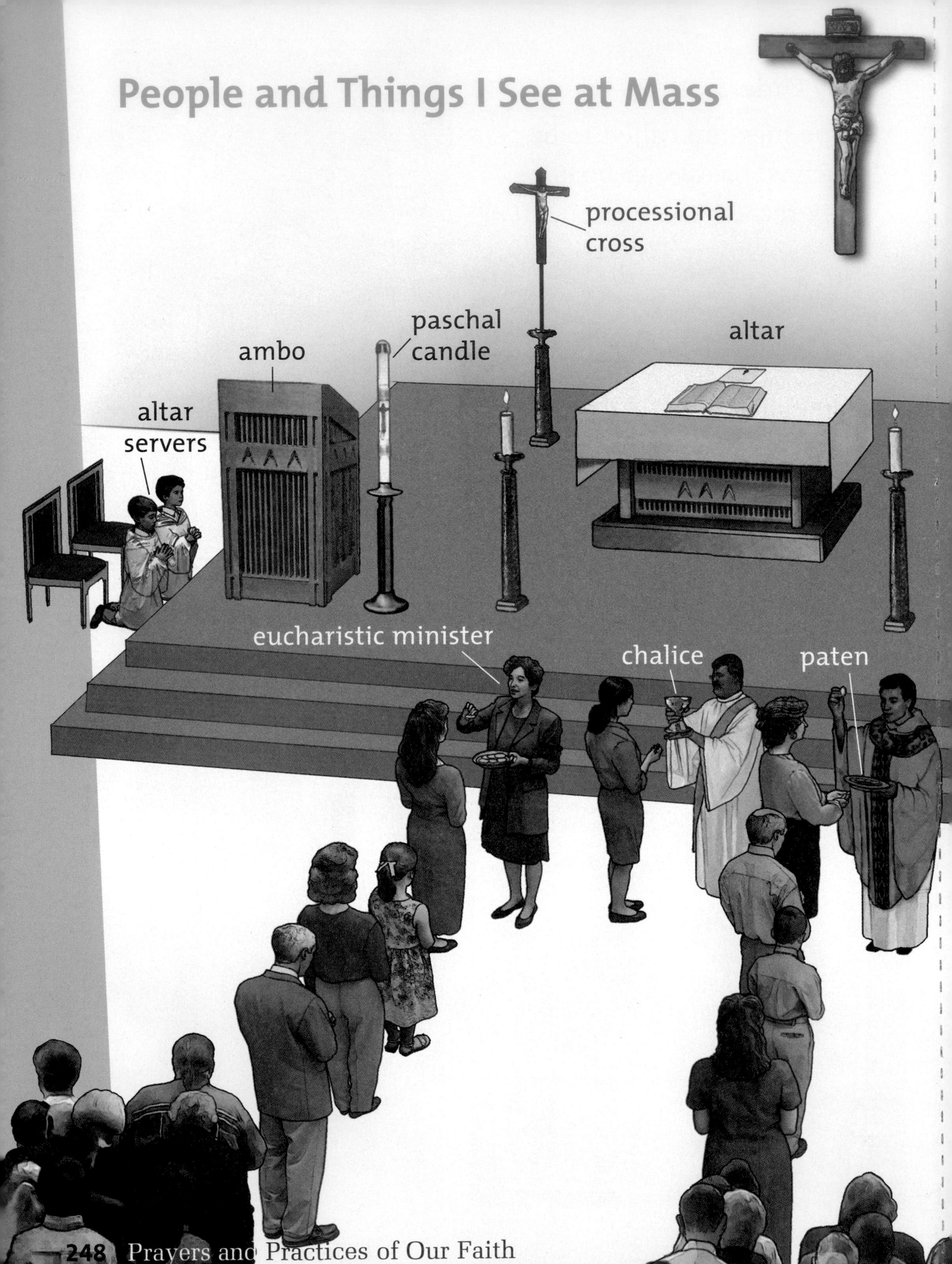

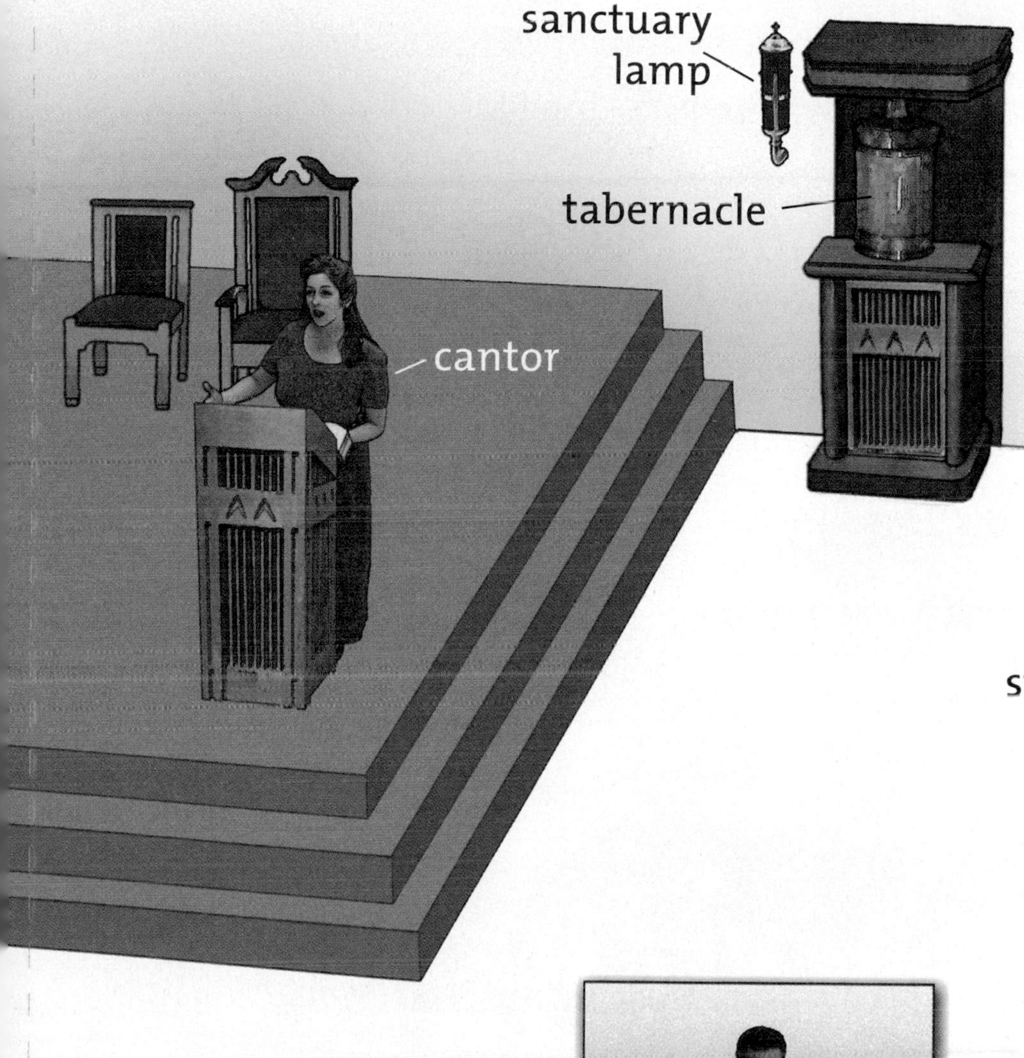

lector

deacon

priest

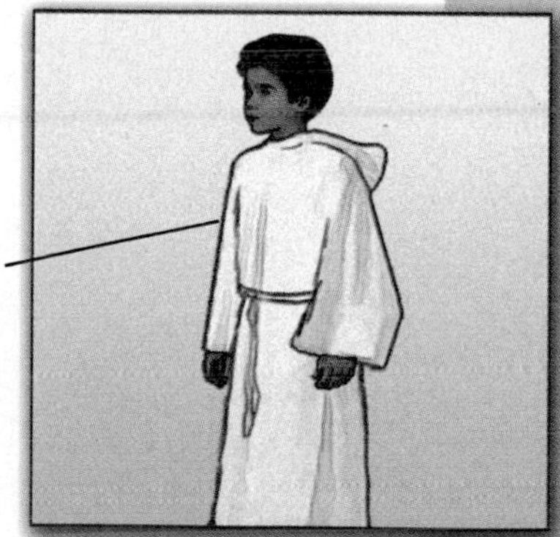

altar server

The Ten Commandments

Rules keep us safe. Rules help us to live in peace. God gives us rules too. We call them the Ten Commandments. We show our love for God by following the Commandments.

1. I am your God; love nothing more than me.
2. Use God's name with respect.
3. Keep the Lord's Day holy.
4. Honor and obey your parents.
5. Treat all human life with respect.

6. Respect married life.
7. Respect what belongs to others.
8. Tell the truth.
9. Respect your neighbors and your friends.
10. Be happy with what you have.

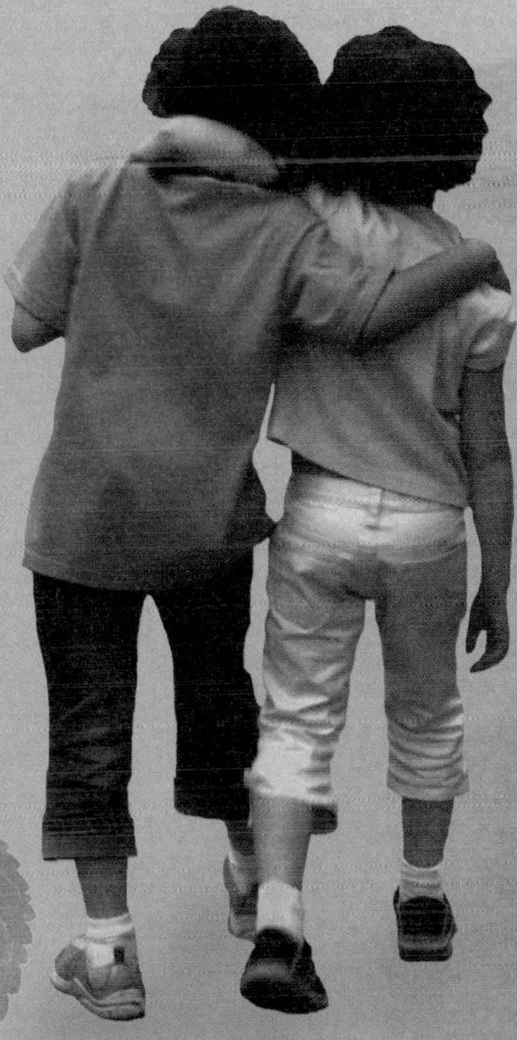

The Great Commandment

People asked Jesus, "What is the most important commandment?" Jesus said, "First, love God. Love him with your heart, soul, and mind. The second is like it: Love your neighbor as yourself."
adapted from Matthew 22:37–39

We call this the Great Commandment.

Showing Our Love for the World

Jesus taught us to care for those in need. The Church teaches us how to do this.

Life and Dignity

God wants us to care for everyone. We are all made in his image.

Family and Community

Jesus wants us to be loving helpers in our families and communities.

Rights and Responsibilities

All people should have what they need to live good lives.

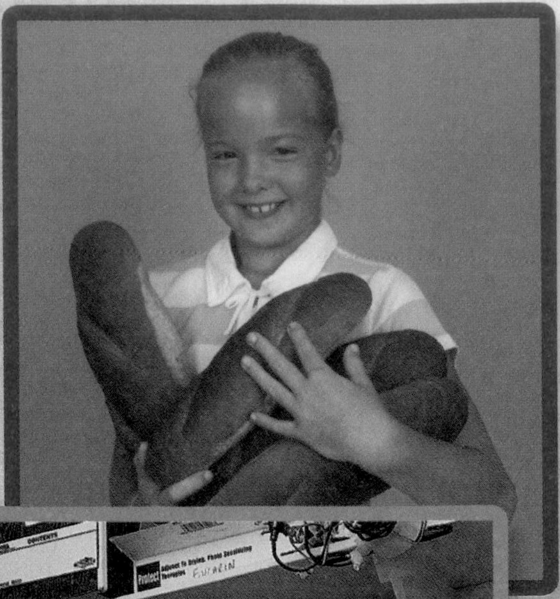

The Poor and Vulnerable

Jesus calls us to do what we can to help people in need.

Work and Workers

The work that we do gives glory to God.

Solidarity

Since God is our Father, we are called to treat everyone in the world as a brother or a sister.

God's Creation

We show our love for God's world by taking care of it.

Song of Love

Chorus

Bm A G A D
Thank you Spir - it for com-ing to me,
Bm A G A G9 (no third)
and for show - ing me how to sing
D
your song of love.
1 3
(to Verse 1)
2 2 A G 2
your song of love.
(to Verses 2 and 3)
3 2 A G 4 (Fine)
your song of love.

continued

Song of Love *(continued)*

Verse 1
Bm G A D
I saw some-one lone-ly by the road,
Em A G D
Some-one my age sad-ly all a-lone.
Bm G A D
I shared my friend-ship and we talked a while.
Em A G A D (to Chorus)
I gave a hand, Je-sus gave back a smile.

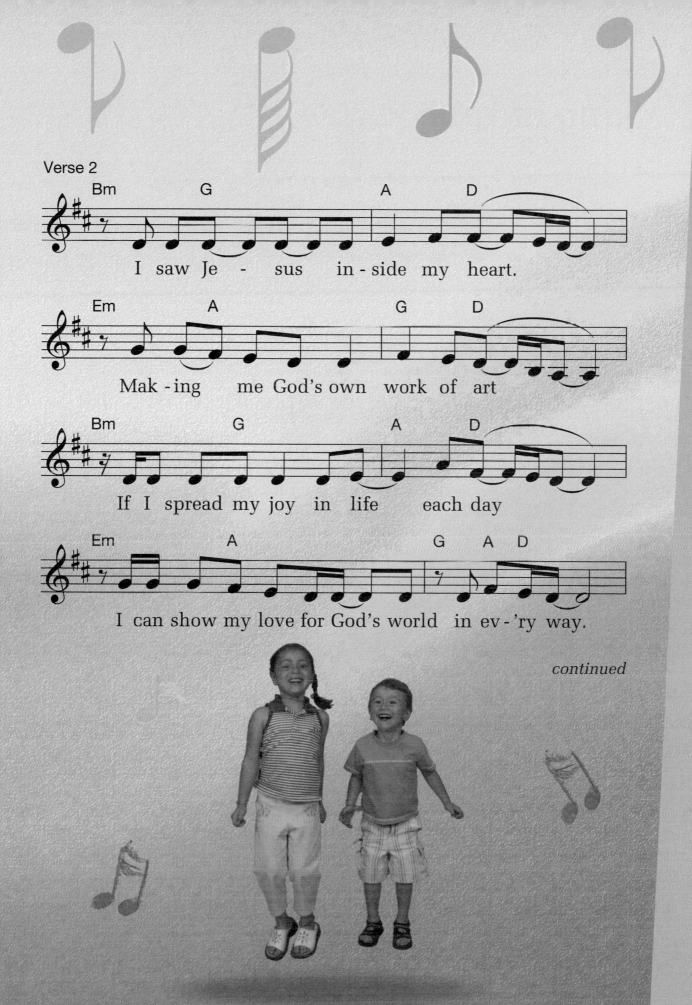

Verse 2
Bm G A D
I saw Je - sus in - side my heart.
Em A G D
Mak - ing me God's own work of art
Bm G A D
If I spread my joy in life each day
Em A G A D
I can show my love for God's world in ev - 'ry way.

continued

Song of Love *(continued)*

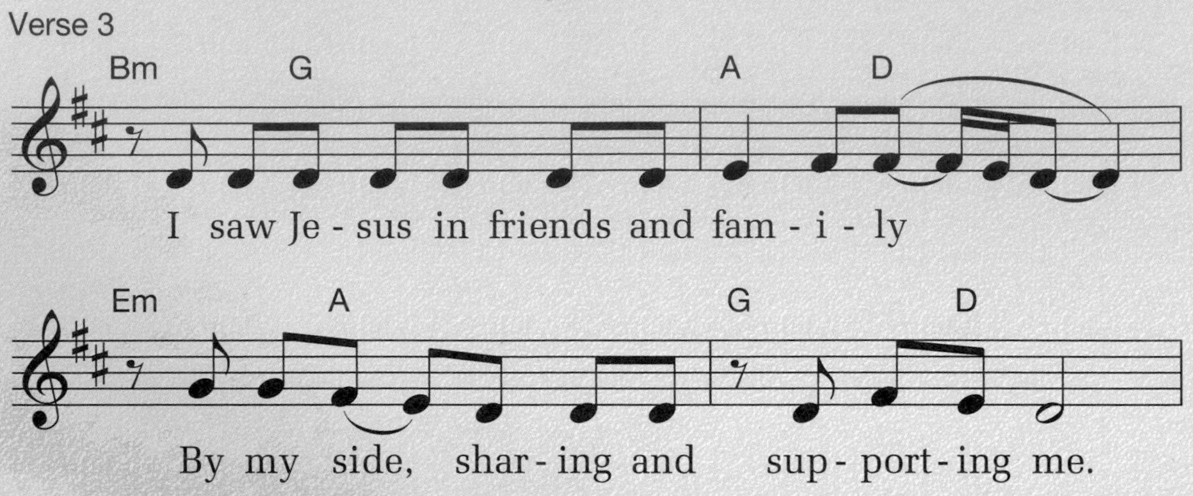
Verse 3
Bm G A D
I saw Je - sus in friends and fam - i - ly
Em A G D
By my side, shar - ing and sup - port - ing me.

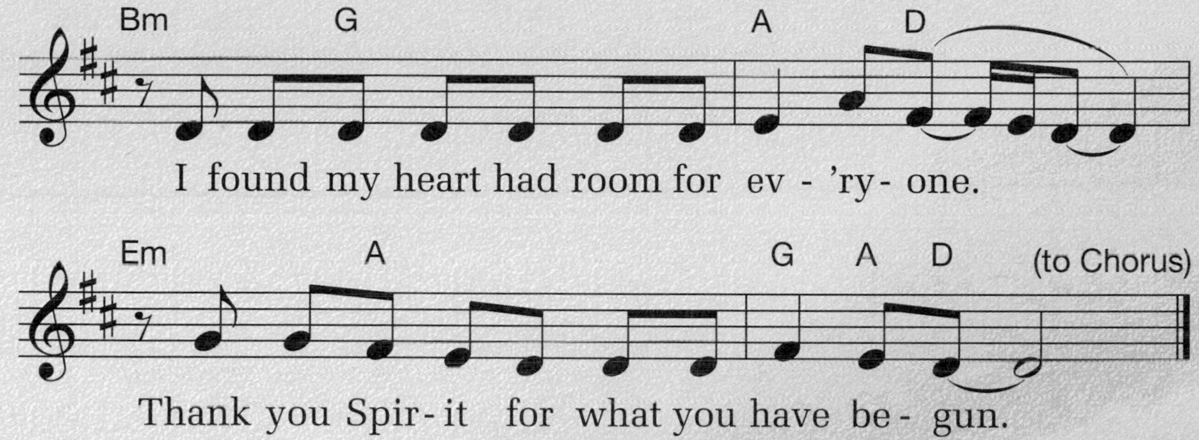
Bm G A D
I found my heart had room for ev - 'ry- one.
Em A G A D (to Chorus)
Thank you Spir- it for what you have be - gun.

Our Father

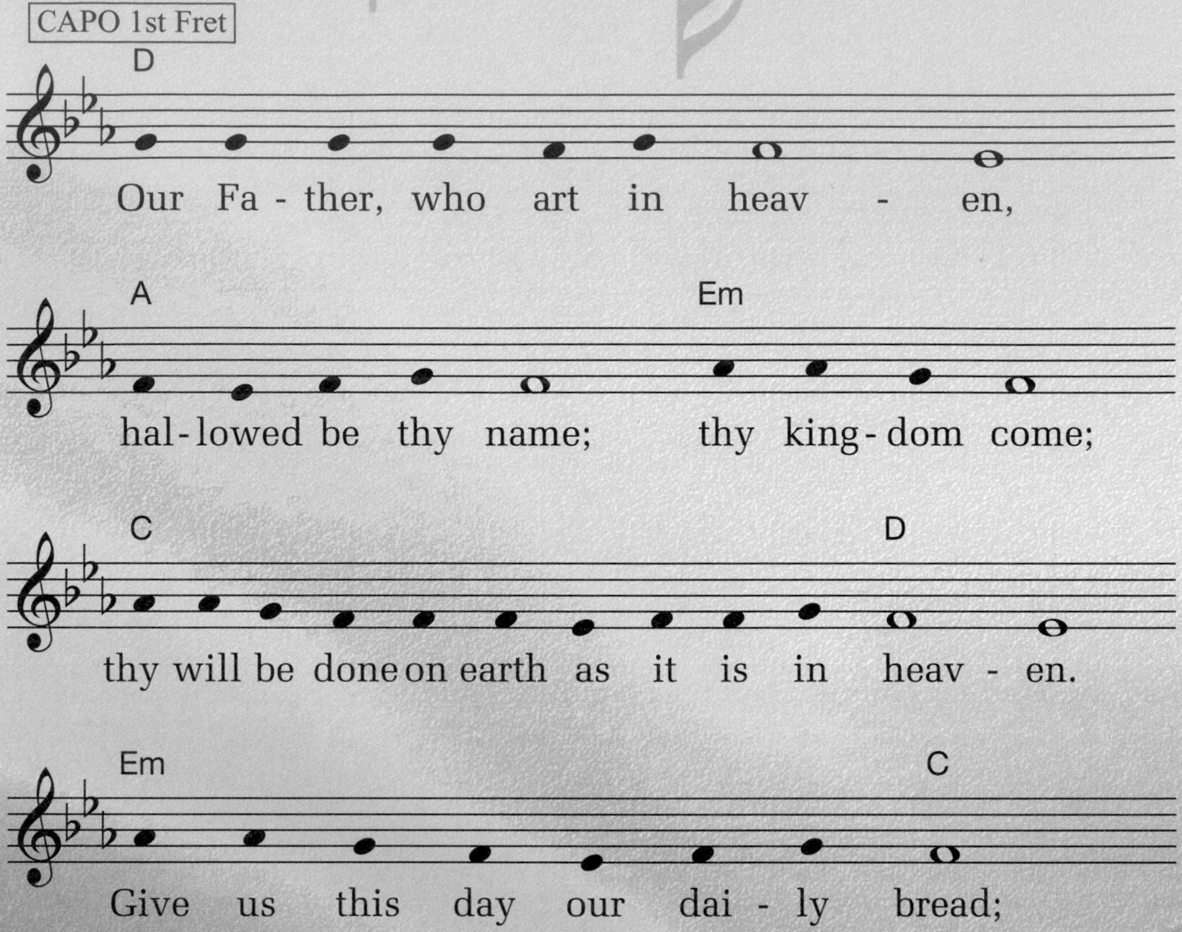
CAPO 1st Fret
D
Our Fa - ther, who art in heav - en,
A Em
hal-lowed be thy name; thy king-dom come;
C D
thy will be done on earth as it is in heav - en.
Em C
Give us this day our dai - ly bread;

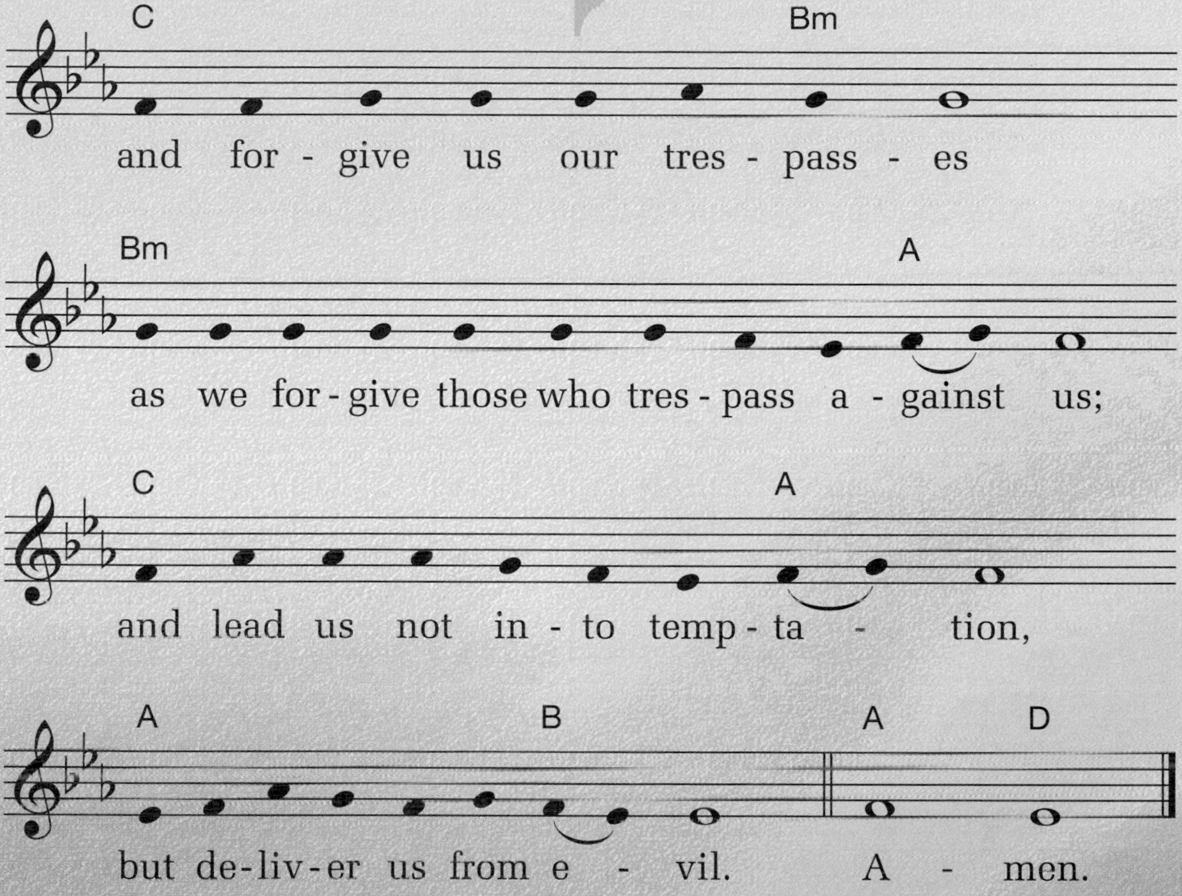

"Our Father," tune from traditional chant.

Come, O Holy Spirit/ Wa Wa Wa Emimimo

1. Come, O Ho - ly Spir - it, come.
2. Come, O Ho - ly Spir - it, come.
3. *Wa wa wa E - mi - mi - mo.*
4. *Wa wa wa E - mi - mi - mo.*

1. Come, Al - might - y Spir - it, come.
2. Come, Al - might - y Spir - it, come.
3. *Wa wa wa A - lag - ba - ra.*
4. *Wa wa wa A - lag - ba - ra.*

1. Come, come, come.
2. Come, come, come.
3. *Wa - o, wa - o, wa - o.*
4. *Wa - o, wa - o, wa - o.*

God Is So Good

1. God is so good, God is so good,
2. God loves me so, God loves me so,
3. God an-swers prayer, God an-swers prayer,
4. God is so good, God is so good,

1. God is so good, He's so good to me.
2. God loves me so, He's so good to me.
3. God an-swers prayer, He's so good to me.
4. God is so good, He's so good to me.

"God Is So Good" from African-American folksong.

This Is the Day

CAPO 1st Fret

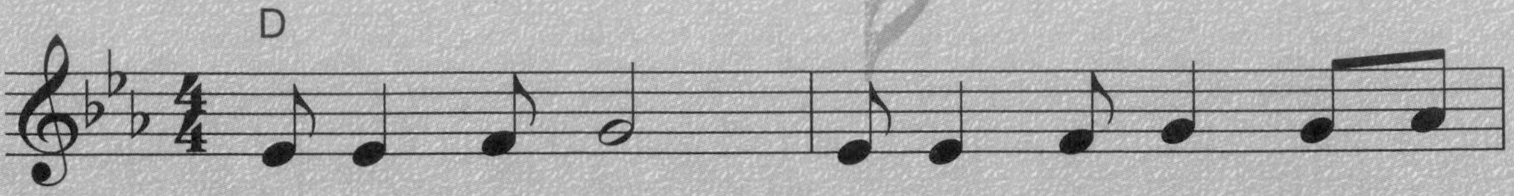

1. This is the day, this is the day that the
2. This is the day, this is the day when he

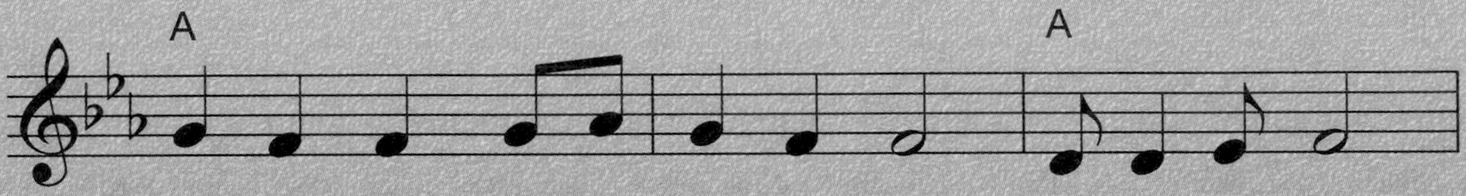

1. Lord has made, that the Lord has made; we will re- joice,
2. rose a - gain, when he rose a - gain; we will re- joice,

1. we will re - joice and be glad in it, and be glad in it.
2. we will re - joice and be glad in it, and be glad in it.

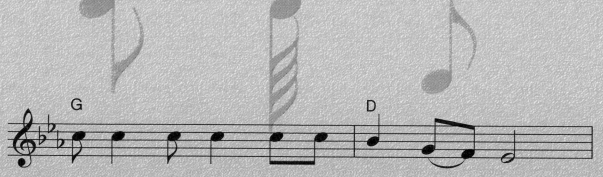

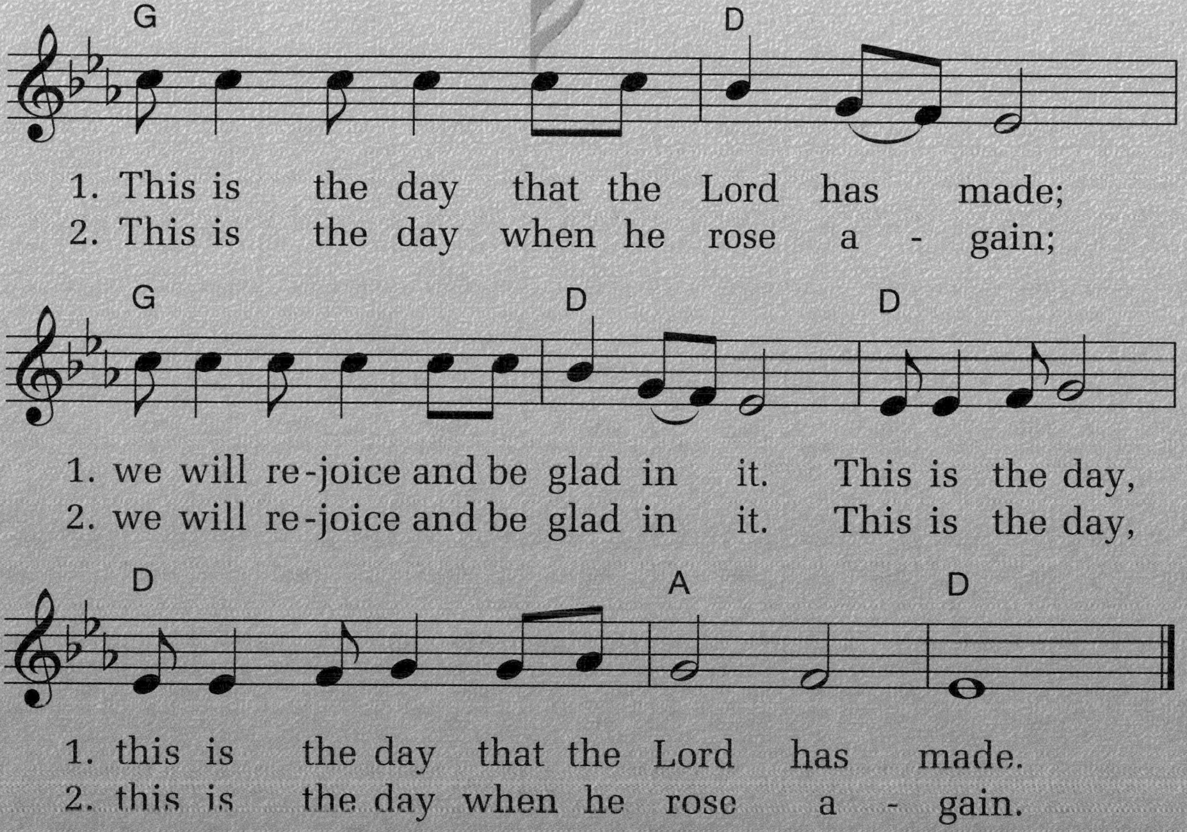
G
D
1. This is the day that the Lord has made;
2. This is the day when he rose a - gain;
G
D
D
1. we will re-joice and be glad in it. This is the day,
2. we will re-joice and be glad in it. This is the day,
D
A
D
1. this is the day that the Lord has made.
2. this is the day when he rose a - gain.

Come All You People

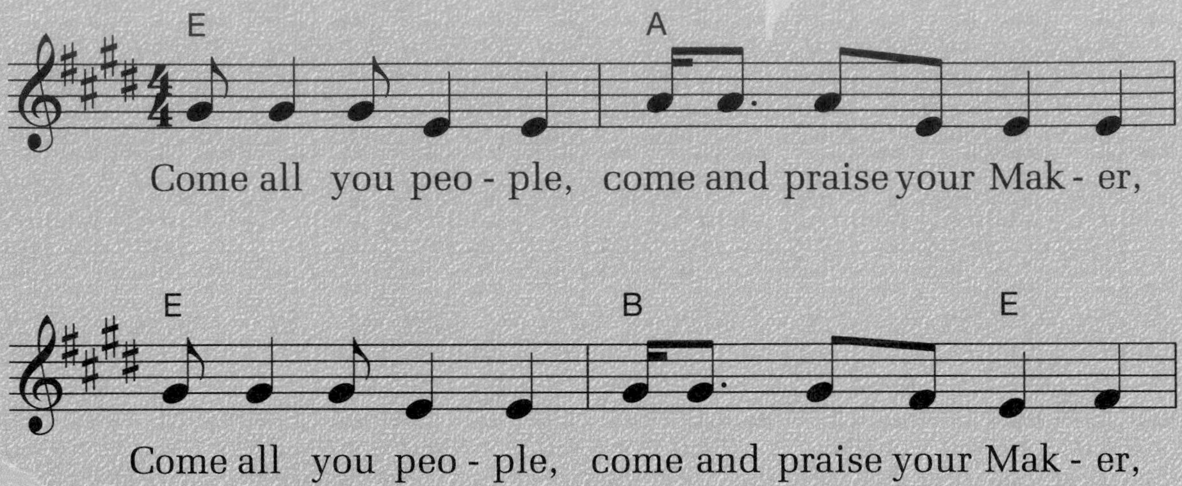
E
A
Come all you peo - ple, come and praise your Mak - er,
E
B
E
Come all you peo - ple, come and praise your Mak - er,

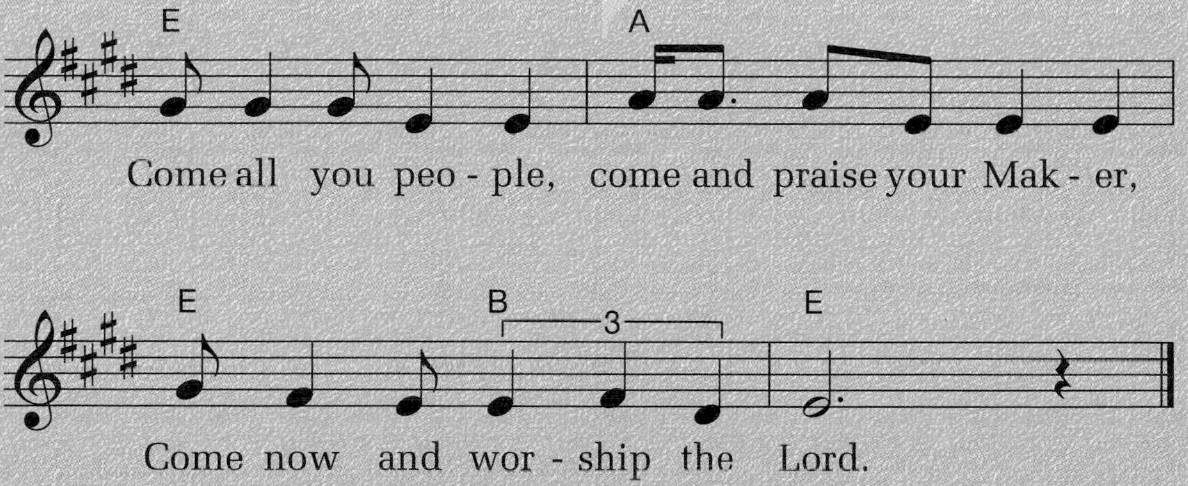
E
A
Come all you peo - ple, come and praise your Mak - er,
E
B
3
E
Come now and wor - ship the Lord.

Guide My Feet

G
G
1. Guide my feet while I run this race.
2. I'm your child while I run this race.
3. Hold my hand while I run this race.
4. Stand by me while I run this race.

G
D
G
1. Guide my feet while I run this race.
2. I'm your child while I run this race.
3. Hold my hand while I run this race.
4. Stand by me while I run this race.

1. Guide my feet while I run this race, For I
2. I'm your child while I run this race, For I
3. Hold my hand while I run this race, For I
4. Stand by me while I run this race, For I

1. don't want to run this race in vain!
2. don't want to run this race in vain!
3. don't want to run this race in vain!
4. don't want to run this race in vain!

"Guide My Feet" from traditional African-American text and tune.

A
B
C

Glossary

A

absolution the forgiveness of God. In the Sacrament of Penance, we say that we are sorry for our sins. Then the priest offers us God's absolution. [absolución]

Advent the four weeks before Christmas. It is a time of joyful preparation for the celebration of Jesus' birth. [Adviento]

Advent wreath

All Saints Day November 1, the day on which the Church honors all who have died and now live with God as saints in heaven. These saints include all those who have been declared saints by the Church and many others known only to God. [Día de Todos los Santos]

All Souls Day November 2, the day on which the Church remembers all who have died as friends of God. We pray that they may rest in peace. [Día de los Muertos]

altar the table in the church on which the priest celebrates Mass. On this table, the bread and wine are offered to God and become the Body and Blood of Jesus Christ. [altar]

altar

ambo a platform from which a person reads the Word of God during Mass [ambón]

Amen the last word in any prayer that we pray. *Amen* means "This is true." We pray "Amen" to show that we really mean the words we have just said. [Amén]

angel a messenger from God [ángel]

Ash Wednesday the first day of Lent, on which we receive ashes on our foreheads to remind us to show sorrow for the choices we make that hurt our friendships with God and others [Miércoles de Ceniza]

B

Baptism the first of the three sacraments by which we become members of the Church. Baptism frees us from original sin and gives us new life in Jesus Christ through the Holy Spirit. [Bautismo]

Beatitudes the eight ways we can behave in order to lead a Christian life. Jesus explains that if we live according to the Beatitudes, we are living as his followers. [Bienaventuranzas]

Bible the written story of God's promise to care for us, especially through his Son, Jesus [Biblia]

bishop a leader in the Church. Bishops teach us what God is asking of us as followers of Jesus today. [obispo]

bishop

Blessed Sacrament the bread that has been consecrated by the priest at Mass. It is kept in the tabernacle to adore and to be taken to the sick and the dying. [Santísimo Sacramento]

Body and Blood of Christ the bread and wine that has been consecrated by the priest at Mass [Cuerpo y Sangre de Cristo]

C

catholic a word that means "all over the world." The Church is catholic because Jesus gave the Church to the whole world. [católico]

Christ a title, like Messiah, that means "anointed with oil." This name is given to Jesus after the Resurrection. [Cristo]

Christmas caroling

Christian the name given to people who want to live as Jesus taught us to live [cristiano]

Christmas the day on which we celebrate the birth of Jesus [Navidad]

Church the name given to the followers of Christ all over the world. Spelled with a small *c*, church is the name of the building in which we gather to pray to God. [Iglesia]

commandment a rule that tells us how to live as God wants us to live [mandamiento]

confession the act of telling our sins to a priest in the Sacrament of Penance [confesión]

Confirmation the sacrament that completes the grace we receive in Baptism [Confirmación]

conscience the inner voice that helps each of us to know what God wants us to do [conciencia]

consecration the making of a thing or person to be special to God through prayer. At Mass the words of the priest are a consecration of the bread and wine. This makes them the Body and Blood of Jesus Christ. [consagración]

consecration

contrition the sadness we feel when we know that we have sinned [contrición]

creation everything that God has made. God said that all of creation is good. [creación]

Creator God, who made everything that is [Creador]

crozier the staff carried by a bishop. This staff shows that the bishop cares for us in the same way that a shepherd cares for his sheep. [báculo]

D

deacon a man who accepts God's call to serve the Church. Deacons help the bishop and priests in the work of the church. [diácono]

disciple a person who is a follower of Jesus and tries to live as he did [discípulo]

E

Easter the celebration of the bodily raising of Jesus Christ from the dead. Easter is the most important Christian feast. [Pascua]

Emmanuel a name that means "God with us." It is a name given to Jesus. [Emanuel]

Eucharist the sacrament in which we give thanks to God for giving us Jesus Christ. [Eucaristía]

examination of conscience thinking about what we have said or done that may have hurt our friendship with God or others [examen de conciencia]

F

faith a gift of God. Faith helps us to believe in God and live as he wants us to live. [fe]

forgiveness the act of being kind to people who have hurt us but then have said that they are sorry. God always forgives us when we say that we are sorry. We forgive others the way God forgives us. [perdón]

Fruits of the Holy Spirit the ways in which we act because God is alive in us [frutos del Espíritu Santo]

G

genuflect to show respect in church by touching a knee to the ground, especially in front of the tabernacle [genuflexión, hacer la]

genuflect

God the Father, Son, and Holy Spirit. God created us, saves us, and lives in us. [Dios]

godparent a witness to Baptism. A godparent helps the baptized person to live as a follower of Jesus. [padrino/madrina de Bautismo]

grace the gift of God given to us without our earning it. Sanctifying grace fills us with God's life and makes us his friends. [gracia]

Great Commandment Jesus' important teaching that we are to love both God and other people [El Mandamiento Mayor]

Holy Communion

H

heaven the life with God that is full of happiness and never ends [cielo]

holy showing the kind of life we live when we cooperate with the grace of God [santa]

Holy Communion the consecrated bread and wine that we receive at Mass, which is the Body and Blood of Jesus Christ [Sagrada Comunión]

Holy Days of Obligation those days other than Sundays on which we celebrate the great things God has done for us through Jesus Christ [días de precepto]

The Holy Family With Lamb

Holy Family the family made up of Jesus; his mother, Mary; and his foster father, Joseph [Sagrada Familia]

Holy Spirit the third person of the Trinity, who comes to us in Baptism and fills us with God's life [Espíritu Santo]

holy water the water that has been blessed. It is used to remind us of our Baptism. [agua bendita]

homily an explanation of God's word. A homily explains the words of God that we hear in the Bible readings at church. [homilía]

hope the trust that God will always be with us. We also trust that he will make us happy now and help us to live in a way that keeps us with him forever. [esperanza]

J

Jesus the Son of God, who was born of the Virgin Mary, died, was raised from the dead, and saves us so that we can live with God forever [Jesús]

Joseph the foster father of Jesus, who was engaged to Mary when the angel announced that Mary would have a child through the power of the Holy Spirit [José]

K

Kingdom of God God's rule over us. We experience the Kingdom of God in part now. We will experience it fully in heaven. [reino de Dios]

L

Last Supper the last meal Jesus ate with his disciples on the night before he died. Every Mass is a remembrance of that last meal. [Última Cena]

Lectionary the book from which the stories from the Bible are read at Mass [Leccionario]

Lectionary

Lent six weeks during which we prepare to celebrate, with special prayers and actions, the rising of Jesus from the dead at Easter. Jesus rose from the dead to save us. [Cuaresma]

liturgy the public prayer of the Church that celebrates the wonderful things God has done for us in Jesus Christ [liturgia]

Liturgy of the Eucharist the second half of the Mass. In this part of the Mass, the bread and wine are consecrated and become the Body and Blood of Jesus Christ. We receive the Body and Blood of Jesus Christ in Holy Communion. [Liturgia de la Eucaristía]

Liturgy of the Word the first half of the Mass. During this part of the Mass, we listen to God's Word from the Bible. [Liturgia de la Palabra]

M

Magnificat Mary's song of praise to God. She praises him for the great things he has done for her and planned for us through Jesus. [Magníficat]

Mary; *The Virgin at Prayer*

Mary the mother of Jesus. She is called "full of grace" because God chose her to be Jesus' mother. [María]

Mass our most important means of praying to God. At Mass we listen to God's Word, the Bible. The bread and wine that has been consecrated becomes the Body and Blood of Jesus Christ. [misa]

Messiah a title, like *Christ*, that means "anointed with oil." *Messiah* also means "Savior." [Mesías]

ministry the service, or work, done for others. Ministry is done by bishops, priests, and deacons in the celebration of the sacraments. All those baptized are called to different kinds of ministry in the liturgy and in serving the needs of others. [ministerio]

moral choice a choice to do what is right. We make moral choices because they are what we believe God wants. [opción moral]

mortal sin a serious choice to turn away from God [pecado mortal]

N

New Testament the story of Jesus and the early Church [Nuevo Testamento]

O

Old Testament the story of God's plan for the salvation of all people [Antiguo Testamento]

original sin the result of the sin of Adam and Eve. They disobeyed God and chose to follow their own will rather than God's will. [pecado original]

P

parable one of the simple stories that Jesus told to show us what God wants for the world [parábola]

parish a community of believers in Jesus Christ who meet regularly to worship God together [parroquia]

penance the turning away from sin because we want to live as God wants us to live (*See* Sacrament of Penance.) [penitencia]

Pentecost the 50th day after Jesus was raised from the dead. On this day the Holy Spirit was sent from heaven, and the Church was born. [Pentecostés]

petition a request of God asking for what we need made with the knowledge that he created us and wants to give us what we need [petición]

pope the bishop of Rome, successor of Saint Peter, and leader of the Roman Catholic Church [Papa]

praise our telling of the happiness we feel simply because God is so good [alabanza]

prayer our talking to God and listening to him in our hearts [oración]

priest a man who accepts God's special call to serve the Church. Priests guide the Church and lead it in the celebration of the sacraments. [sacerdote]

R

reconciliation making friends again after a friendship has been broken by some action or lack of action. In the Sacrament of Penance, we are reconciled with God, the Church, and others. [Reconciliación]

Resurrection the bodily raising of Jesus Christ from the dead on the third day after he died on the cross [Resurrección]

rite the special form followed in celebrating each sacrament [rito]

S

sacrament the way in which God enters our life. Through simple objects such as water, oil, and bread, Jesus continues to bless us. [sacramento]

Sacrament of Penance the sacrament in which we celebrate God's forgiveness of our sins when we say to the priest that we are sorry for them [sacramento de la Penitencia]

Sacraments of Initiation the sacraments that make us members of God's Church. They are Baptism, Confirmation, and the Eucharist. [sacramentos de iniciación]

Sacrament of Penance

Sacrifice of the Mass the sacrifice of Jesus on the cross. We remember Jesus' sacrifice every time we celebrate Mass. [Sacrificio de la misa]

saint a holy person who has died as a true friend of God and now lives with God forever [santo]

Savior Jesus, the Son of God, who became human to make us friends with God again. The name *Jesus* means "God saves." [Salvador]

sin a choice we make that hurts our friendships with God and with other people [pecado]

T

tabernacle the container in which the Blessed Sacrament is kept so that Holy Communion can be taken to the sick and the dying [sagrario]

tabernacle

temptation a thought or feeling that can lead us to disobey God. Temptation can come either from outside us or inside us. [tentación]

Ten Commandments the ten rules that God gave to Moses. The Ten Commandments sum up God's law and show us how to live as his children. [Diez Mandamientos]

trespasses acts that harm others [ofensas]

Trinity the mystery of one God, existing in three persons: the Father, the Son, and the Holy Spirit [Trinidad]

V

venial sin a choice we make that weakens our relationship with God or other people [pecado venial]

Glosario

A

absolución perdón de Dios. En el sacramento de la Penitencia, después de que decimos que nos arrepentimos de nuestros pecados, el sacerdote nos ofrece la absolución de Dios. [absolution]

Adviento las cuatro semanas antes de la Navidad. Es una época de alegre preparación para la celebración del nacimiento de Jesús. [Advent]

agua bendita agua que ha sido bendecida. Se usa para recordarnos nuestro Bautismo. [holy water]

alabanza nuestra expresión de la alegría que sentimos sencillamente porque Dios es muy bueno. [praise]

altar mesa en las iglesias en la que el sacerdote celebra la misa. En esta mesa, se ofrece a Dios el pan y el vino para que se conviertan en el Cuerpo y Sangre de Jesucristo. [altar]

ambón plataforma desde donde una persona proclama la Palabra de Dios durante la misa. [ambo]

Amén última palabra de todas las oraciones que rezamos. *Amén* quiere decir "es verdad". Decimos *Amén* para mostrar que lo que acabamos de decir va en serio. [Amen]

ángel mensajero de Dios. [angel]

Antiguo Testamento la historia del plan de Dios para la salvación de toda la gente. [Old Testament]

B

báculo vara que lleva un obispo. Al llevar esta vara, un obispo muestra que cuida de nosotros de la misma forma en que un pastor cuida sus ovejas. [crozier]

Bautismo el primero de los tres sacramentos mediante los cuales pasamos a ser miembros de la Iglesia. El Bautismo nos libera del pecado original y nos da una vida nueva en Jesucristo por medio del Espíritu Santo. [Baptism]

Biblia historia escrita de la promesa que hizo Dios de cuidar de nosotros, especialmente a través de su Hijo, Jesús [Bible]

Bienaventuranzas ocho formas en que podemos comportarnos para poder llevar una vida cristiana. Jesús nos explica que, si vivimos según las Bienaventuranzas, vivimos como sus seguidores. [Beatitudes]

C

católica quiere decir "universal". La Iglesia es católica porque Jesús la ha dado al mundo entero. [catholic]

cielo vida con Dios que está llena de felicidad y que nunca termina. [heaven]

conciencia nuestra voz interior que nos guía a cada uno a hacer lo que Dios nos pide. [conscience]

confesión acto de contar nuestros pecados al sacerdote en el sacramento de la Penitencia. [confession]

Confirmación sacramento que completa la gracia que recibimos en el Bautismo. [Confirmation]

consagración el hacer a una cosa o persona especial ante los ojos de Dios por medio de la oración. En la misa, las palabras del sacerdote son una consagración del pan y el vino. Esto los convierte en el Cuerpo y Sangre de Jesucristo. [consecration]

contrición tristeza que sentimos cuando sabemos que hemos pecado. [contrition]

creación todo lo que hizo Dios. Dios dijo que toda de la creación es buena. [creation]

Creador Dios, quien hizo todo lo que existe. [Creator]

cristiano nombre dado a todos los que quieren vivir como Jesús nos enseñó. [Christian]

Cristo título, que al igual que "El Mesías", significa "el ungido con aceite". Se le dio este título a Jesús después de la Resurrección. [Christ]

Cuaresma las seis semanas en las que nos preparamos, con oraciones y acciones especiales, a celebrar en la Pascua la Resurrección de Jesús de entre los muertos. Jesús resucitó para salvarnos. [Lent]

Cuerpo y Sangre de Cristo pan y vino que han sido consagrados por el sacerdote en la misa. [Body and Blood of Christ]

D

Día de los Muertos el 2 de noviembre, día en que la Iglesia recuerda a todos los que han muerto como amigos de Dios. Oramos por ellos para que descansen en paz. [All Souls Day]

Día de Todos los Santos el 1° de noviembre, día en que la Iglesia recuerda a todos los muertos que pasaron a ser santos y ahora viven con Dios en el cielo. Éstos son todos los muertos que han sido declarados santos por la Iglesia y otros que sólo Dios conoce. [All Saints Day]

diácono varón que acepta la llamada de Dios a servir a la Iglesia. Los diáconos ayudan al obispo y a los sacerdotes en el trabajo de la Iglesia. [deacon]

días de precepto aquellos días que no sean domingos en que celebramos las grandes cosas que Dios ha hecho por nosotros a través de Jesucristo. [Holy Days of Obligation]

Diez Mandamientos diez reglas que Dios dio a Moisés que resumen la ley de Dios y nos muestran cómo vivir como hijos suyos. [Ten Commandments]

Dios Padre, Hijo, y Espíritu Santo. Dios nos creó, él nos salva, y vive en nosotros. [God]

discípulo persona que sigue a Jesús y trata de vivir de la misma forma en que él vivió. [disciple]

E

Emanuel nombre que significa "Dios con nosotros". Es el nombre que se le da a Jesús. [Emmanuel]

esperanza confianza de que Dios estará siempre con nosotros. También confiamos en que él nos dará la felicidad ahora y nos ayudará a vivir de una forma que nos mantendrá con él para siempre. [hope]

Espíritu Santo tercera Persona de la Trinidad, que viene a nosotros en el Bautismo y nos llena de la vida de Dios. [Holy Spirit]

Eucaristía sacramento en el cual damos gracias a Dios por habernos dado a Jesucristo. [Eucharist]

examen de conciencia el pensar sobre lo que hemos dicho o hecho que pudo haber dañado nuestra amistad con Dios y con otras personas. [examination of conscience]

F

fe don de Dios. La fe nos permite creer en Dios y vivir de la forma en que él quiere que vivamos. [faith]

frutos del Espíritu Santo forma en que actuamos porque Dios vive en nosotros. [Fruits of the Holy Spirit]

G

genuflexión, hacer la forma de mostrar respeto en la iglesia doblando una rodilla y haciéndola tocar el suelo, sobre todo cuando estamos delante del sagrario. [genuflect]

gracia don de Dios que se nos da gratuitamente. La gracia santificante nos llena de la vida de Dios y nos hace sus amigos. [grace]

H

homilía explicación de la Palabra de Dios. Una homilía explica las palabras de Dios que oímos durante las lecturas de la Biblia en la iglesia. [homily]

I

Iglesia nombre que se le da a los seguidores de Jesús por todo el mundo. Si se escribe con "i" minúscula, para referirse al edificio donde nos reunimos para orar. [Church]

J

Jesús Hijo de Dios, que nació de la Virgen María, murió, fue resucitado de entre los muertos, y nos salva para que podamos vivir con Dios para siempre. [Jesus]

José padre adoptivo de Jesús, que estaba desposado con María cuando el ángel anunció que ella tendría un hijo por obra del poder del Espíritu Santo. [Joseph]

L

Leccionario libro del cual se leen en la misa los relatos de la Biblia. [Lectionary]

liturgia oración pública de la Iglesia que celebra las maravillas que Dios ha hecho por nosotros en Jesucristo. [liturgy]

Liturgia de la Eucaristía la segunda de las dos partes de la misa. En esta parte se consagran el pan y el vino, que se convierten en el Cuerpo y Sangre de Jesucristo. Luego, recibimos el Cuerpo y Sangre de Cristo en la Sagrada Comunión. [Liturgy of the Eucharist]

Liturgia de la Palabra la primera de las dos partes de la misa. Durante esta parte, escuchamos la Palabra de Dios en la Biblia. [Liturgy of the Word]

M

Magníficat canto de María de alabanza a Dios. Ella lo alaba por las grandes cosas que ha hecho por ella y los grandes planes que ha hecho para nosotros a través de Jesús. [Magnificat]

mandamiento regla que nos muestra cómo vivir de la forma en que Dios quiere que vivamos. [commandment]

El Mandamiento Mayor enseñanza importante de Jesús de amar a Dios y a los demás. [Great Commandment]

María madre de Jesús. Se le dice "llena de gracia" porque Dios la eligió para ser madre de Jesús. [Mary]

Mesías título dado a Jesús, igual que "Cristo", que quiere decir "ungido". Mesías significa también "Salvador". [Messiah]

Miércoles de Ceniza primer día de Cuaresma en el que se nos coloca ceniza en la frente para que nos acordemos de mostrar arrepentimiento por decisiones que hemos tomado que dañan nuestra amistad con Dios y los demás. [Ash Wednesday]

ministerio servicio u obra que se hace para otros. Lo hacen los obispos, sacerdotes, y diáconos en la celebración de los sacramentos. Todos los bautizados son llamados a distintos tipos de ministerio en la liturgia y en el servicio a las necesidades de los demás. [ministry]

misa la forma más importante de rezar a Dios. En la misa escuchamos la Palabra de Dios en la Biblia. El pan y el vino consagrados se convierten en el Cuerpo y Sangre de Jesucristo. [Mass]

N

Navidad día en que se festeja el nacimiento de Jesús. [Christmas]

Nuevo Testamento la historia de Jesús y la Iglesia antigua. [New Testament]

O

obispo uno de los líderes de la Iglesia. Los obispos nos enseñan lo que Dios nos pide hoy como seguidores de Jesús. [bishop]

ofensas daño que hacemos a otros. [trespasses]

opción moral elegir hacer lo que está bien. Elegimos opciones morales porque son lo que creemos que Dios quiere. [moral choice]

oración hablar con Dios y escucharlo en nuestro corazón. [prayer]

P

padrino/madrina de Bautismo testigo de Bautismo. El padrino o la madrina ayuda al bautizado a vivir como seguidor de Jesús. [godparent]

Papa el obispo de Roma, sucesor de San Pedro, y cabeza de la Iglesia Católica Romana. [pope]

parábola una de las narraciones sencillas que Jesús contaba que nos muestran lo que Dios quiere para el mundo. [parable]

parroquia comunidad de creyentes en Jesucristo que se reúne regularmente a dar culto a Dios. [parish]

Pascua celebración de la Resurrección de Jesucristo de entre los muertos. La Pascua es la fiesta cristiana más importante. [Easter]

pecado decisión que daña nuestra amistad con Dios y con los demás. [sin]

pecado mortal decisión grave que nos aparta de Dios. [mortal sin]

pecado original resultado del pecado de Adán y Eva. Ellos desobedecieron a Dios y decidieron seguir su propia voluntad y no la de Dios. [original sin]

pecado venial decisión que debilita nuestra relación con Dios y los demás. [venial sin]

penitencia apartarnos del pecado porque queremos vivir de la forma en que Dios quiere que vivamos. (*Véase* sacramento de la Penitencia). [penance]

Pentecostés cincuenta días después de la Resurrección de Jesús. En este día, el Espíritu Santo fue enviado del cielo y nació la Iglesia. [Pentecost]

perdón acción bondadosa con personas que nos han hecho daño pero que después nos dicen que están arrepentidas. Dios siempre nos perdona cuando decimos que estamos arrepentidos. Nosotros perdonamos a los demás al igual que Dios nos perdona. [forgiveness]

petición pedir a Dios lo que necesitamos, porque él nos ha creado y quiere darnos lo necesario. [petition]

R

reconciliación volver a ser amigos después de haber roto una amistad por alguna acción o falta de acción. En el sacramento de la Penitencia, nos reconciliamos con Dios, la Iglesia, y los demás. [reconciliation]

reino de Dios dominio de Dios sobre nosotros. Experimentamos hoy el reino de Dios en parte, pero lo experimentaremos por completo en el cielo. [Kingdom of God]

Resurrección el regreso a la vida del cuerpo de Jesucristo al tercer día después de haber muerto en la cruz. [Resurrection]

rito acciones especiales que hacemos para celebrar cada sacramento. [rite]

S

sacerdote varón que ha aceptado un llamado especial para servir a la Iglesia. Los sacerdotes guían a la Iglesia y presiden la celebración de los sacramentos. [priest]

sacramento forma en que Dios entra en nuestra vida. Por medio de objetos sencillos, como el agua, el aceite, y el pan, Jesús sigue bendiciéndonos. [sacrament]

sacramento de la Penitencia sacramento en el cual celebramos el perdón de Dios de nuestros pecados cuando decimos a un sacerdote que nos arrepentimos de ellos. [Sacrament of Penance]

sacramentos de iniciación sacramentos que nos hacen miembros de la Iglesia de Dios. Son tres: Bautismo, Confirmación y Eucaristía. [Sacraments of Initiation]

Sacrificio de la misa sacrificio de Jesús en la cruz. Lo recordamos cada vez que celebramos la misa. [Sacrifice of the Mass]

Sagrada Comunión el pan y el vino consagrados que recibimos en la misa son el Cuerpo y Sangre de Jesucristo. [Holy Communion]

Sagrada Familia familia compuesta por Jesús, su madre María y su padre adoptivo, José. [Holy Family]

sagrario lugar donde se guarda el Santísimo Sacramento para que la Sagrada Comunión pueda ser llevada a los enfermos y a los moribundos. [tabernacle]

Salvador Jesús, el Hijo de Dios, que se hizo hombre para que volvamos a ser amigos con Dios. El nombre *Jesús* quiere decir "Dios salva". [Savior]

santa tipo de vida que vivimos cuando cooperamos con la gracia de Dios. [holy]

Santísimo Sacramento pan que ha sido consagrado por el sacerdote en la misa. Se guarda en el sagrario para su adoración y para ser llevado a los enfermos y a los moribundos. [Blessed Sacrament]

santo persona virtuosa y ejemplar que ha muerto estando en amistad con Dios y que ahora vive con él para siempre. [saint]

T

tentación pensamiento o sentimiento que puede llevar a desobedecer a Dios. La tentación puede venir de fuera o de dentro de nosotros mismos. [temptation]

Trinidad misterio de la existencia de un Dios en tres Personas: Padre, Hijo, y Espíritu Santo. [Trinity]

U

Última Cena último comida que compartieron Jesús y sus discípulos la noche antes de que muriera. Cada misa es un recordatorio de esa Última Cena. [Last Supper]

Acknowledgments

Excerpts from the English translation of *Rite of Baptism for Children* © 1969, International Commission on English in the Liturgy, Inc. (ICEL); excerpts from the English translation of *The Roman Missal* © 1973, ICEL; excerpts from the English translation of *Book of Blessings* © 1988, ICEL. All rights reserved. Used with permission.

Excerpts from *The New American Bible with Revised New Testament and Psalms* Copyright © 1991, 1986, 1970 Confraternity of Christian Doctrine, Inc., Washington, DC. Used with permission. All rights reserved. No portion of the *New American Bible* may be reprinted without permission in writing from the copyright holder.

26 "Prayer Rock." Author unknown, from *Big Book of Ideas for Children's Faith Formation,* Our Sunday Visitor, Inc.: Huntington, IN. Used with permission.

186 "I Lie Down This Night" from *Carmina Gadelica,* Scottish Academic Press, collected and translated by Alexander Carmichael.

Illustration

Doron Ben Ami: 6, 11, 12–13, 14, 22–23, 25, 37, 40, 49, 51, 60–61, 67, 70, 83, 107, 151, 163, 164–165, 166, 167, 175, 187, 188–189, 190, 191, 197, 212–213, 215, 217, 219, 229, 233, 236, 239, 248–249, 253

Tristan Elwell: 1, 2, 7, 41, 42, 81, 82, 87, 121, 122, 161, 162

Vitali Konstantinov: 201

David LaFleur: 2–3, 20, 28, 30–31, 35, 36, 42, 44, 45, 46, 52–53, 68, 69, 75, 82–83, 84–85, 92, 93, 100, 108–109, 115, 122, 124, 132, 140–141, 148–149, 157, 162, 163, 172–173, 180–181, 195, 202–203, 204, 208–209, 216–217, 221, 224, 225, 235, 240, 241, 242, 243, 252, 256–271

Monica Liu: 223

Olwyn Whelan: 23, 31, 43, 63, 71, 86, 87, 95, 101, 102, 109, 124, 141, 143, 150, 156, 158, 174, 183, 209, 228, 232

Photography

Unless otherwise acknowledged, photos are the property of Loyola Press. When there is more than one picture on a page, credits are supplied in sequence, left to right, top to bottom. Page positions are abbreviated as follows: (t) top, (m) middle, (b) bottom, (l) left, (r) right, (bkgr) background, (ins) inset, (cl) clockwise from top, right.

UNIT 1: 3 © Ariel Skelley/CORBIS. **4** (all) © Phil Martin Photography. **5** (b,r) Leonidas Orellano Castro. **6** (t,r and b,r) © Phil Martin Photography. **7** (t,r) © David Young-Wolff/PhotoEdit. **8** (bkgr) © Phil Martin Photography. **9** © Phil Martin Photography. **10** (t,r) Hamburg Kunsthalle, Hamburg, Germany/Bridgeman Art Library; (m,r) © Phil Martin Photography. **15** © Passionist Research Center/John T. Render, C.P., D.Min. **16** © Jeff Greenberg/PhotoEdit. **17** © Peter Correz/Getty Images. **18** (t,l) © Wilson McLean/The Newborn Group; (b,l) © Myrleen F. Cate/PhotoEdit; (b,r) © Tony Freeman/PhotoEdit. **24** © Tony Freeman/PhotoEdit. **26** (t,l) photodisc/Getty Images; (m,r) © Kristen Miller/The Stock Illustration Source; (b,r) photodisc/Getty Images. **27** © Don Smetzer/PhotoEdit. **28** (bkgr) © Phil Martin Photography. **29** (t) © Barbara Stitzer/PhotoEdit; (m) © Richard Hutchings/PhotoEdit; (b) © David Young-Wolff/PhotoEdit. **32** © Phil Martin Photography. **33** © Paul Redman/Getty Images. **34** (t,r) © Kristen Miller/The Stock Illustration Source; (m,r) © Laura Dwight/PhotoEdit; (b,l) Vivian Cherry's Photo Gallery; (b,r) © Myrleen F. Cate/PhotoEdit. **35** © Elio Ciol/CORBIS. **36** photodisc/Getty Images; all other photos, © Phil Martin Photography. **37, 38, 39** (bkgr) © Phil Martin Photography. **40** © David Young-Wolff/Getty Images.

UNIT 2: 43 (l) © David Young-Wolff/PhotoEdit; (r) photodisc/Getty Images. **47** Leonidas Orellano Castro. **48** © Phil Martin Photography. **50** (t,r) Dover Publications; (m,l) photodisc/Getty Images. **54** (b,r) © Phil Martin Photography. **55** (t,l) © Andy Sachs/Getty Images/PictureQuest. **56** © Felicia Martinez/PhotoEdit. **57** © Myrleen F. Cate/PhotoEdit. **58** (t and b,l) © Reuters News Media Inc./CORBIS. **59** (t,l) © Paul Sisul/Getty Images; (t,r) © Syracuse Newspapers/Al Campanie/The Image Works. **63** (t,r and m,l) © Phil Martin Photography. **64** (bkgr) © Phil Martin Photography. **65** photodisc/Getty Images. **66** (t,l) Skjold Photography; (b,r) © PBNJ Productions/CORBIS. **72** © O'Brien Productions/CORBIS. **74** (t,r) © The Crosiers/Gene Plaisted OSC; (m,l) © Jose Luis Pelaez, Inc./CORBIS; (b,r) © Michael Newman/PhotoEdit. **73, 75, 77, 80** © Phil Martin Photography.

UNIT 3: 83 (t) © Jeffry Myers/Stock Boston/PictureQuest; (b) © Mark Gibson Photography. **86** (t and m) © Passionist Research Center/John T. Render, C.P., D.Min. 89 (b,l and r) © Phil Martin Photography; (b,m) © ImageState-Pictor/PictureQuest. **90** (t,l) © Michael Newman/PhotoEdit; (b,l) © Frank Siteman/PhotoEdit. **94** (t,l) © David Oliver/Getty Images; (t,r) © Phil Martin Photography; (b,m) © Journal Courier/Image Works. **96** © David Stover. **97** © Syracuse Newspapers/Brian Phillips/The Image Works. **98** (t,r) © The Crosiers/Gene Plaisted OSC ; (b,l) Courtesy of Notre Dame University Archives. **99** (t,l) © Ellen Senisi/The Image Works; (t,r) © Myrleen F. Cate/PhotoEdit; (b,r) © Bill Lai/The Image Works. **101** © Denis Felix/ Getty Images. **103** (t and m,r) © Phil Martin Photography. **104** © Jeff Greenberg/PhotoEdit. **105** © Ghislain & Marie David de Lossy/Getty Images. **106** (t,r) © The Crosiers/Gene Plaisted OSC; (b,l) photodisc/Getty Images; (b,r) © Myrleen F. Cate/PhotoEdit. **110** © Leanne Temme/photolibrary/PictureQuest. **111** © Arte & Immagini srl/CORBIS. **110, 111** (bkgr) © Phil Martin Photography. **112** Bridgeman Art Library. **113** © Tony Freeman/PhotoEdit. **114** (t,l) © Hamilton Reed Armstrong; (b,r) George A. Lane, S.J. **119** (bkgr) © Phil Martin Photography. **120** © Hornback c/o Kienzle/eStock Photo/PictureQuest.

UNIT 4: 123 (b,r) © Richard Hutchings/PhotoEdit. **126** © Phil Martin Photography. **127** (all) © The Crosiers/Gene Plaisted OSC. **153** (b) © Tony Arruza/CORBIS. **128** © Dennis Curran/Index Stock Imagery/Picture Quest. **130** (t,l) Courtesy Old Christ Church; (m,r) © Tony Freeman/PhotoEdit; (b,r) © Myrleen F. Cate/PhotoEdit. **131** (m,l) © Phil Martin Photography. **133** (t) © The Crosiers/Gene Plaisted OSC. **136** © Richard Shock/Getty Images. **137** © Phil Martin Photography. **138** (t,l) © Robert Brenner/PhotoEdit; (m,l) © Hulton-Deutsch Collection/CORBIS; (m,r) © The Crosiers/Gene Plaisted OSC; (b,r) © Myrleen F. Cate/PhotoEdit. **144** (bkgr) © Phil Martin Photography. **145** © Image State-Pictor/PictureQuest. **146** (t,l) © Myrleen F. Cate/PhotoEdit; (m,r) © Jeff Greenberg/PhotoEdit; (b,r) photodisc/Getty Images. **150** (t,r) © Doug Mazell/Index Stock Imagery/Picture Quest; (m,r) © Chip Henderson/Index Stock Imagery/PictureQuest. **151** (m,l) © Bob Daemmrich/Image Works. **152** © Richard Price/Getty Images. **153** photodisc/Getty Images. **154** (m,l) © David Young-Wolff; (m,r) © Spencer Grant; (b,l) Myrleen F. Cate/(all) PhotoEdit. **155** (t,r) © Vecto Verso/eStock Photo/PictureQuest; (m) Phil Martin Photography. **156** (t,l) © The Crosiers/Gene Plaisted OSC. **159** (bkgr) © Phil Martin Photography.

UNIT 5: 163 © Phil Martin Photography. **170** (t,l) © Tony Freeman/ PhotoEdit; (b,l) © Margaret Ross/Stock Boston/PictureQuest; (b,r) © Mary Kate Denny/PhotoEdit. **176** © Yu Jiade. **177** © Kim Fowler Photography/ eStock Photography/Picture Quest. **178** "Children of the World Illustrate the Bible" by MallMedia Publishing www.bible2000.com; (m,l) © Myrleen F. Cate/PhotoEdit; (b,r) © Michael Newman/PhotoEdit. **182** (t,r) © Ken Huang/Getty Images (b) © China Tourism Press/Getty Images. **186** (t,l) © David Young-Wolff/PhotoEdit; (m,r) © Jeff Greenberg/PhotoEdit. **187** (living creatures except children) © Phil Martin Photography. **192** © Phil Martin Photography. **196** (t,r) © James Frank/Stock Connection/ PictureQuest; (b,r) © Arthur Tilley/Getty Images. **198, 199** © IT International/ eStock Photo/PictureQuest. **200** © Mark Scott/Getty Images.

UNIT 6: 202 (t,r) photodisc/Getty Images; (m,r) © Grant V. Faint/Getty Images; (b,r) © Vie de Jesus Mafa, www.jesusmafa.com; (b,l) Art Resource, NY. **206** © Phil Martin Photography. **207** © Zaki Baboun/Christian Asian Art Association. **210** © Leanne Temme/photolibrary/PictureQuest. **211** (l) Phil Martin Photography; (t,r) © IFA/eStock Photo/PictureQuest; (b,r) © Myrleen F. Cate/PhotoEdit. **214** and **218** © Phil Martin Photography. **220** (t) © He Qi. **222** © PicturesNOW. **223** © Monica Liu. **226** (and ins) Bridgeman Art Library. **227, 230** John Nava/© Los Angeles Cathedral of Our Lady of the Angels.

END MATTER: 231, 232, 233 (bkgr) © Phil Martin Photography. **239** (t) © Phil Martin Photography. **244** (m,r) © Phil Martin Photography. **245, 246, 247** (t,r and b,l) © Phil Martin Photography. **247** (b,r) © Maureen Collins Photography.

GLOSSARY: 273 (t) © Mary Kate Denny/PhotoEdit. **275** © Kindra Clineff/Index Stock Imagery. **276** © The Crosiers/Gene Plaisted, OSC. **278** (t) © The Crosiers/Gene Plaisted; (b) © Archivo Iconografico, S.A./ CORBIS. **280** © Christie's Images/CORBIS. **282** © The Crosiers/Gene Plaisted, OSC.

All photographs (except tabletop/still life) not listed above were taken by Phil Martin Photography.

All tabletop/still life photographs not listed above were taken by Greg Kuepfer.